MI-I01077647

Magic by Design:

How to create your own practical magic workings that get results

Magic by Design:
How to create your own practical magic workings that get results

Taylor Ellwood

Portland, Oregon

Magic by Design: How to create your own practical magic workings that get results
by Taylor Ellwood
© 2020 first edition

All rights reserved, including the right to reproduce this book, or portions thereof, in any form.

The right of Taylor Ellwood to be identified as the author of this work has been asserted by him in accordance with the Copyright, Designs and Patents Act, 1988.

Cover Art: Mark Reid
Editor: Kat Bailey

Set in Consolas and Book Antiqua

ME0016
ISBN 9781671297081

Magical Experiments Publication
http://www.magicalexperiments.com

Other Non-Fiction Books by Taylor Ellwood

The Process of Magic
Pop Culture Magic 2.0
Pop Culture Magic Systems
Space/Time Magic
Space/Time Magic Foundations
Inner Alchemy
Manifesting Wealth
Magical Identity
The Book of Good Practices (With Bill Whitcomb)
Creating Magical Entities (With David Michael Cunningham & Amanda Wagener)
A Magical Life
Mystical Journeys
Magical Movements
A Magical Stillness
The Magic of Art

Coming Soon

The Inner Alchemy of Breath and Sound
The Magic of Writing
The Inner Alchemy of Failure
How to Work with Spirits

Fiction by Taylor Ellwood

Learning How to Fly
Learning How to be Free
The Zombie Apocalypse Call Center

Coming Soon

Learning How to be a Hero
Secret Missions of the Zombie Apocalypse Call Center

Learn How Magic Works!

Free E-books available on my website
Magicalexperiments.com

Whether you want a learn a simple 4 step process for creating a magical working, or discover how take your fandom and turn it into a spiritual practice, or learn simple breath meditations that enhance your life, or discover how to turn probabilities I have free e-books available for you that will teach you how magic works and how to get consistent results with it. Visit magicalexperiments.com/free books and download your free e-book today!

Dedication

To archangel Khamael who gave me this book to write and to RJ Stewart for helping me learn new perspectives on practical magic.

Acknowledgements

I want to acknowledge the following people who have supported this book with questions, commentary and perspectives: Janet Callahan, Jacki Chuculate, Amandeep Singh, Alison Chicosky, and Gemma Young. As always Mark Reid produced an outstanding book cover and my dearest Kat did an excellent job of editing. I also appreciate the magical experiments community which continues to prompt some excellent conversations and explorations of magic.

Table of Contents

Introduction

I wrote this book to show you how to develop your own workings and modify other peoples' magical workings, because there is a gap in the discipline of magic. There are lots of cookie cutter books being published with spells and techniques galore, but what is lacking is a solid explanation and understanding of how magic works. And the result runs counter to the purpose of magic itself. Instead of empowering people, which is what ought to happen when a person practices magic, people are spoon fed magical spells and techniques without in-depth instruction of how to create their own workings or a concise, clear explanation of how the spell and/or technique is supposed to work. I've written this book, as well as the others in this series, to fill in that gap.

My goal is to empower you as a magician by helping you develop the critical skills that allow you to graduate beyond merely replicating the work of other people, to actually developing your own workings. While this book is a short, concise work, it is purposely written that way to help you focus on the content. I don't believe in needless complexity or filler for the sake of having more pages.

This book came about because one evening in the Magical Experiments Facebook group, a member shared how frustrated they were with their magical practice. It had become boring to them. They explained that they were doing a variety of workings, offerings, and other practices, and nothing was happening. Worse, they had been doing all of this for a year and it had become drudge work that they didn't look forward to doing.

Imagine not looking forward to doing magical work...

Actually I can't imagine that, but maybe you can. And if you can, then this book is for you. Or if you just want to create your own magical workings that get results this book is also for you, because I'm going to share with you my methods for designing your own magical workings. And if you're interested in doing long term magical workings or creating your own system of magic, this book will provide some valuable insights that can help you with those goals. Learning both of these skills will help you become a more proficient magician and teach you a perspective of magic that allows you to take apart magical workings and put them back together with your own variations. Some people will tell you that modifying the magical work of other people can't be done or that creating your own magical working requires years of experience, but while I agree that a certain foundational knowledge is needed, I also think once you have that knowledge you can learn a lot by actually experimenting with magic and discovering for yourself what really makes magic work. It doesn't take a lot of time either, provided you're willing to apply yourself daily to your magical work. I started experimenting with magic within a year of first practicing. And so this is book is written with that in mind, because I want to help you become a better magician.

Doing just that has helped me develop my own unique magical workings and resulted in the various systems of magic I've written about and shared with other magicians. Had I only stuck to the conventional and orthodox explanations of magic, I never would have developed those unique systems.

The evolution of magic won't be found by endlessly repeating what other people have done while being bored out of our gourds with the work we're doing. The evolution of magic happens when we introduce creativity, imagination, and play into our magical practices, and ask ourselves what we can do to truly make the magic our own. And that's what I'm going to teach you so that you can develop your own workings and modify the workings of other people and get better results.

This book is written with the expectation that you already have some experience with magical practice. It's not a 101 book and the audience, i.e. you, has ideally practiced magic and gotten some experience under your belt as a result.

When you understand how magic works, then you become much more versatile as a magician. You can develop your own magical workings, take other magical workings apart, and put them back together. The ability to do all of this is something that can be learned. It just requires taking on a different perspective with your magical work, one which opens you to challenging what you know by discovering what you can learn.

I started experimenting with magic within a year of practicing because I was curious about what could be done, and because it became very evident to me that either key information was missing from the books I was learning from, or that the author didn't have a clear understanding of how magic works. Regardless of which it was, I knew the only way I could resolve the problems I was discovering was to come up with my own solutions. Ever since then I've continually modified the work of other magicians, while also developing my original workings. I've also encouraged other magicians to do the same with my work, because while there are specific principles at work in a given process of magic, a lot of magic can be personalized.

It's my hope that this book will encourage you in your pursuit of magic as a discipline, while also empowering you to strike out on your own. If magic is to continue to evolve as a discipline, we must do more than just blindly repeat what is presented to us. Instead we must critically examine what is already there, learn from it and improve on it, while also developing our own original work. That way lies the path to becoming a true magician.

Taylor Ellwood
November 2019
Portland, OR

Chapter 1: Design and Process

I've been designing original magical workings and modifying other peoples' magical workings from almost the beginning of my magical practice. It's not a skill someone taught me, but rather something I developed on my own, informed in large part by my insatiable curiosity and tendency to ask lots of questions and then go seeking answers. Not everyone has that same curiosity however, and this book is written with that in mind. I can teach you the skills for designing your own original workings and/or modifying other people's magical workings so you can get better results. You may wonder whether you truly can develop an original working, or if you should dare to modify an existing one, so let me address those concerns first before we get into the practical work.

I think anyone can develop an original magical working or modify an existing one, provided a few factors are considered. Do you have the foundational knowledge and experience with magic to create an original magical working or modify an existing one? If you don't have that foundational knowledge and experience then it will be hard, if not downright impossible, to create an original magical working or modify an existing one. The reason is you won't have an understanding of the principles and process of magic and how magic ought to work, which necessarily will inform how you create an original magical working or modify someone else's working[1]. You really only get that understanding from doing the actual work and having experiences that shape and temper your understanding of magic and how it ought to work.

A second factor to consider is what your overall experiences and knowledge are, and how they can be applied to inspire your magical work. What this means is that ideally you have a variety of interests and background to draw upon that can help inspire your magical work. For example, I have interests in a variety of topics that aren't considered occult, but nonetheless inspire my magical workings significantly. I find

---

[1] See my book The Process of Magic, which provide further information in the principles and process of magic.

that sometimes a person may have an in-depth knowledge and experience of the occult, but not really have knowledge or experience of anything else, which leads to tunnel vision when it comes to magic because you're so indoctrinated to what can ultimately be considered limited perspectives on life and your magical practice. There's a myth that occultists and magicians are open-minded, but I haven't really found that to be the case. If anything, your average occultist is much like any other person, albeit interested in magic. There's nothing wrong with that, per se, but if you really want to broaden your horizons you'll necessarily need to step outside of what you already know in order to discover what you can learn. In turn, what you learn can be applied to what you know and produce interesting outcomes in your life, your magical practice, and anything else which is of interest to you.

The third factor is that you must be curious. Really, this factor goes hand in hand with what I mentioned above, but it cannot be said enough that curiosity is essential for developing an approach to magic and life that encourages experimentation and the drive to have new experiences. Without curiosity we dull our minds and lose one of our most powerful tools: the imagination. Without imagination you cannot create anything original, for it's in the imagination that you'll discover the seeds of original thinking and perspective that will enable you to embrace the unconventional and apply it to your magical work. And in this book, that's what we're really exploring.

I've always embraced the unconventional because conventional approaches within any discipline will only get you so far before you discover their limitations. Conventional approaches have value, which is why I recommend acquiring a foundational knowledge of magic (and any other discipline you want to apply to magic). Having that foundational knowledge will help you become acquainted with what you can do with conventional solutions. More importantly, it will also help you become acquainted with what you can't do and what the limitations are around conventional methods. When you encounter those limitations, that's when you'll have to explore unconventional approaches in order to either bypass the limitations or get rid of them altogether.

An unconventional approach to magic embraces the realization that drawing on the disciplines outside of the occult is necessary for revolutionizing the occult and creating novel and original magical workings. Some occultists will balk at that notion, arguing that what's in the occult works just fine and why should they draw on outside disciplines at all. And to that argument I'll say do what works for you, but if you're interested in creating original magical workings or modifying other people's workings, then what is required is that you step outside the conventional boundaries of occultism and embrace the unconventional. This can be found by exploring other disciplines and asking ourselves how we can apply those disciplines to magic. It is this embracing of the unconventional that has allowed me to develop multiple working systems of magic that get results not only for myself, but many other people using those systems every day.

In order to adopt an unconventional approach to magic, I'm going to share some principles with you that draw on creativity and imagination. These principles can help us uncover novel solutions and adopt perspectives that enable us to create original workings and modify existing ones. We're also going to learn the process for approaching all magical workings, that if mastered will help you become a better magician and get better results.

Challenge What You Know by Discovering What You Can Learn

One of the blinders every person possesses is what they know. What we know blinds us because you know it and knowing something brings with it certain assumptions that can cause you to take a situation for granted. I know X and X ought to apply to this situation, because I know it does. But does X really apply? When we use what we know to make assumptions about what may happen, most times we will likely be correct, but there are occasions where we will not be correct, because we don't have the full picture.

You can see why what you know can be problematic, because what you know can cause you to ignore relevant information that could change what you would otherwise do.

That's one reason to challenge what you know, but the other reason is this: if you want to develop original workings, you need to challenge yourself and what you know. You need to test what you know against what you can learn to discover. The opportunity that requires an original solution, unbounded by conventional thinking.

Challenging what you know means that you can never take what you know for granted. Ideally, there will always be an element of doubt that you'll employ to help you challenge what you know in favor of keeping yourself open to experience and what it can teach you. By doubting what you know, you keep yourself open to discovering possibilities and new information that may inform the magical workings you develop, as well as how you handle the situation you're in. And by keeping yourself open to alternate perspectives, you embrace the novel and find the opportunity that lies between the gap of what you know and the solution you're seeking.

So how do you challenge what you know?

Ask Questions and Entertain Possibilities

When you ask questions you provide an outlet for curiosity, which is necessary if you're going to develop innovative approaches to magic (or anything else for that matter). You challenge what you know by asking questions, even the simplest questions, where the answer seems obvious. By asking those questions you give yourself permission to discover the actual answer, instead of assuming you already have it.

When I ask questions, what it really allows me to do is engage my imagination and entertain different possibilities that could be relevant to the magical working I'm developing. I usually end up ruling out some of the possibilities, but by considering them through the questions I ask, I can at least determine why I would them out. And even if I rule a possibility, it's still available if I want to bring it back into play at a later time.

I recommend that when you're either modifying an existing working or developing a new one, that you write your questions down, as well as the answers you come up with. This provides you a quick reference guide to your own thought process around the magical work you're developing. Additionally, if you find that the ideas you've developed aren't working, you can go back and review what your initial thought process was and use it to help you either develop an alternative solution or refine your current attempt.

Up until this point everything is theory. And theory only becomes practice when you...

Apply Ideas into Practice and Test, Test, Test

Until an idea is applied, it's just conjecture and speculation about what could happen. Anyone can theorize about what will happen if an idea is turned into a practical application, but if it's never applied it doesn't matter. When you've developed an original working or modified someone else's working, you must do something with that work. So create the magical working and then apply it to reality and see what results you get.

It's really as simple as that, though it's also as complicated as that. Do the magical working. Record what happens, and then keep doing the working. Refine it and improve it. Test everything you do so you understand what's happening and why and so you can improve on what you've created.

So how do you turn an idea into an actual magical working?

First, define your result. What is it this working will help you accomplish? How will this working change your life? When you define the result, you define the process that is used to create the result. The result is also what you use to help you discover the gap. If an existing magical working can't help you get what you want, that's when you need to create an original magical working of your own.

After you've defined the result, create your step by step process that will help you realize that result. Each step of the process is something you must do in order to achieve your result. Not every step will necessarily involve magical work, but magical work will likely be part of your process, and, as such, you want to use your process to develop the steps that you'll undertake in your magical work.

Finally, do the magical work and keep a record of what you did and what result you obtained. If you didn't get exactly what you wanted, do some troubleshooting and refine your magical working accordingly[2].

What I've shared above is the basic framework that you can apply to any magical working, but it is especially essential when you're developing your own original magical workings, because it provides you a foundation from which to do those workings and a way to track your work and improve on it. If you can master this basic framework, you'll find that magic becomes a lot easier to practice because what you bring to it is the necessary rigor and focus that will help you achieve results and improve the workings that you're doing.

What about Design?

The title of this chapter is process AND design. I've spoken to the basic process of magic, but let's explore the design aspects of magic. When you think about the word design, what comes to mind? Perhaps it's an artistic blueprint or an outline for a book. Those are examples of design, but design, overall, is an approach that allows you to organize various elements of magic and determine what is needed, versus what can be let go of.

The design approach to magic utilizes the principle of essentialism, which focuses on using what is only absolutely essential to making your magic work. What's essential will vary from person to person, because one person may find that using a specific tool or herb or whatever else to be essential to their magical working, and another person may not. Neither person is wrong, nor is either of their approaches to magic wrong. What we need to recognize is that design allows us to see the entire board and pick from it what we need in order to create a magical working or modify one.

When we apply perspectives of design to magic, what we're doing is learning how to critically examine what can go into a magical working, as well as what can be left out. We're also learning an aesthetic appreciation of magic that allows us to

---

[2] If you're not sure how to troubleshoot your magical workings, see my book How to Troubleshoot Magic.

not just consider the functionality of a working, but also the elegance of it. This is why I consider the aesthetics of magic to be an important principle that informs how magic will work: We use the aesthetics to help us understand and apply magic to the world around us. This is why, for some people, a ritual uniform is important. It helps them get into the right space and time to do the magical work. It's why candles or herbs or other things may be essential for some and not for others. When we marry design to process what we get is a seamless magical experience, while also learning how to design our own original magical processes. Most of all what we learn is that magic is a variable process. What works for some people won't work for other people, but fortunately we can tailor our magical experiences accordingly provided we understand what is essential for us to be able to do magical work.

The Aesthetics of Magic

A book on designing your own magical workings and modifying other peoples' workings isn't complete without a consideration of the aesthetics of magic. The aesthetics of magic is an important element of magical design, because we don't merely want to focus on the functionality of our magical workings, but also the appearance and experience of the working.

If you look at a given magical working, there is one key aspect which ought to be observed and appreciated: how the experience of the magical working changes you while you are doing the working. In my mind, that is the aesthetics of magic, right there. The aesthetics describes the elegance of magic and how the experience transforms you, and what is necessary for you, the magician, to achieve that experience.

Magical components, tools, chants, etc., have an aesthetic function that pairs up with the role they perform in the working. That aesthetic function creates the atmosphere, the space, the time, and the altering of one's consciousness. Without the aesthetic you miss something fundamental in your magic. Applying this particular lens to your magical work can be quite helpful in enabling you to create an experience that is transformative.

As you design a magical working or modify it, think about the act of doing the magic and how it gets you into the precise mental, spiritual, and physical space where you access the magic. The aesthetics are part of what gets you there because they are the specific trappings you use to make yourself receptive to the magic. You'll want to think about those trappings and how best to use them in the magical workings you design and modify to help you get the results you want.

Conclusion

In the next chapter what we're going to explore is how to modify an existing magical working. I'll share a few case studies where I've done just that and walk you through my process for how and why I modified the magical working. I want you to learn how to modify an existing working, because learning how to do that will also help you start developing original workings. It'll help you learn the necessary creative thinking you'll need in order to create original magical workings and magical systems of your own.

This book is a concise book by design because I want to focus on only the essential and get rid of the distractions. As you'll discover, that level of focus will help you do amazing things and that's what I want for you. Let's get started!

Chapter 2: How to Modify Magical Workings

You can modify any existing magical working that is already out there.

Read that sentence again.

I asked you to read that sentence again because I find that a lot of people think you shouldn't modify existing magical workings. You'll hear reasons such as, "It's dangerous to modify a magical working," or "You can't modify a magical working, because you don't know what the original person did with that magical working," or "If you don't use those specific components or tools, will the magic working even work?"

These reasons will hold many an aspiring magician back because they're treated as laws, when in fact what they really demonstrate is a profound misunderstanding of how magic works. That misunderstanding has come about because of the way magic is typically presented. Open up your average spell book and you see lots of esoteric terms thrown around, with vague warnings about what not to do, and yet no clear explanation for why. Or, alternately, you see shallow explanations that don't really explain how magic works, but just tell you to do magic. Neither approach is useful if you really want to become an effective magician.

So let's throw all those reasons out. You can and should modify existing magical workings. In fact, I want you to start doing that from this day forward. But we don't want to be sloppy about modifications. We shouldn't modify a magical working just for the sake of modifying it (unless you really want to experiment). The modification we make to an existing magical work ought to make sense and help us get a better result.

First, I want to discuss how to simplify and optimize your magical practice, while also considering the question how much simplification is too much simplification. I'm a magic minimalist myself, but I also think that going overboard with minimalism can actually take away from the magical experience if the magician isn't careful. When designing your own magical workings, this is an important variable to consider in the design of your magic. Let's first consider the argument for simplifying magical work as well as the argument against it.

Why Would You Even Want to Simplify a Magical Working?

The advantage of simplifying a magical working is that you're stripping away the aspects of the magical working that aren't essential to making it work. As I've alluded to above, and in my other works a lot of magical workings are weighed down with unnecessary requirements. When we recognize that a magical working can be stripped of what's unnecessary, we afford ourselves the opportunity to discover how to streamline the magical work.

A simplified magical working uses only what's necessary and questions every single action, component, etc. included in the magical working. When you take a minimalist approach to magic, you work with what you have access to instead of trying to acquire everything that might be required. And, as a result, you discover what really is required and what's optional, because if you can make the magic work without everything required and get the same results, then you've discovered what you really need.

An example of such a magical working are my evocation portals. Your typical approach to evocation is elaborate and requires that you collect a lot of materials in order to do the evocation. The argument is that without all of the materials included, the evocation won't be effective. I've discovered otherwise with my evocation portals, which don't involve a lot of elaborate work, but serve as a way to evoke a spirit.

What I do is strip away the ceremonial regalia and tools, the evocation triangle and the circle, and focus instead on the relationship I wanted to develop with the spirit. I do an initial invocation to determine if the spirit and I will work together, and then a second one where I channel the spirit while painting the sigil of the spirit. The painting becomes the evocation portal created by the spirit and I together, and it can be used to evoke the spirit whenever desired.

This is a minimalist approach which focuses on streamlining the evocation process in favor of achieving results, without getting caught up in needless complexity. Of course, grimoire purists will argue that my approach to evocation isn't as effective as their approach, but given that I've gotten real results, I think the proof is in the pudding.

Why make magic more complicated than it needs to be? The reason we simplify magic is because we don't need complexity. Complexity muddies the water and when we got caught up in that complexity, we lose sight of the magic and of the work we truly need to do.

Why You Shouldn't Simplify a Magical Working

Of course, there will be people who will argue that you shouldn't simplify a magical working, and that by doing so you take away critical parts of the working that are necessary to accomplish the working. Let's consider that argument for a moment.

It can be argued that there are specific reasons for everything included in a magical working, and that without those things included, the magic working isn't the same. Simplifying the magic, if that argument is valid, makes the magic less effective and makes the result something different than what it ought to be.

There is some validity to this argument. You can simplify a magic working too much or take something out of it that shouldn't be taken out, but let's get clear on why the magic is diluted. It's not the simplification itself that is the issue. It's the underlying approach to magic that's the issue.

The magical workings where I've observed a difference in result have typically been done by people who argue that magic is all in the head, that it's a psychological phenomenon and doesn't really have an effect on the world around them. One wonders why they even bother practicing magic when they hold such a ridiculous perspective! Simplifying magic in this way does dilute it because you are trying to categorize magic into something it isn't and then apply that category to your life, limiting the effect that magic can have.

"But Taylor, if magic is real, how is my limiting it to a psychological phenomenon causing it to be diluted? Shouldn't the magic affect me beyond a psychological way, if your argument is correct?"

Nice trick question. Magic responds to your limitations and operates in those limitations because of you how approach it. So, if you treat magic as a psychological force, it'll oblige you. If, on the other hand, you approach it from an experiential perspective, opening yourself to experience and discovering how the magic can move you and through you, you'll discover a very different reality. This is why magicians the world over have different experiences with magic, because you have some who choose to limit themselves, while others stay open to the possibilities.

If you open yourself to the magic and allow it to work through you, you can have some amazing experiences. But it requires a willingness to let go of preconceptions and expectations about how magic ought to work. Instead, you need to challenge what you know by discovering what you can learn, and that happens when we let go of the need to control magic through categorization and focus instead on being present with the experience.

The other times I've observed a markedly different result is when people try to create short cuts for a magical working without fully understanding what they're changing. When you simplify magic, you need to understand what you're changing and why before you make changes to a working. I sometimes see people make changes out of whim, without really determining why the change would work or how it would still generate the same result. If you're going to simplify magic, then you need to understand how that simplification will still make the magical work either get the same result or a better result.

I shared my evocation example earlier, so let's use it again. I did traditional evocations a few times, and what I discovered was that I didn't like that approach because of how it constrains the spirit. The relationship created between you and the spirit is antagonistic, in my opinion, because you're trying to control the spirit and treat it as if it's something that will attack you.

I made the choice to simplify evocations, but also to radically change the overall relationship. I asked myself if it was possible to have a mutually beneficial relationship with a spirit and based on my overall experiences determined it was. With that understanding, I decided to do away with the traditional approach to evocation, focusing instead on creating a working based on mutual respect. I wasn't creating short cuts to the evocation process, but instead coming up with a new process that could get similar, if not better results, without the consequences that seem to occur with traditional evocation.

I don't recommend simplifying a magical work unless you have clearly understood reasons for doing so, and you're willing to test them and see if the simplification makes the magical work easier. The point of making any changes to a magical working isn't to create short cuts, but to actually improve your understanding and connection to the magic. The reason we simplify is because getting rid of needless complexity actually improves the quality of the magical work we do.

Simplifying the Magic Working

The most common modification is the choice to simplify a magical working by taking away unneeded elements of the working that are making it needlessly complex. The majority of spell books out there have examples of needlessly complex magical workings with a long list of components that are needed, actions that need to be taken, and chants that need to be said. Maybe the person putting the original spell together really did need all of that stuff, but we shouldn't apply a one size fits all mentality to our magical work.

Consequentially what we can do is get rid of the needless complexity by stripping out the elements that we don't need. Again, this will vary from person to person. For some, the entire list of components might be what needs to go, while for others, it might be getting rid of some of the actions or the chant. A given magical working shouldn't be treated as a sacred cow, but instead should be something you can modify as you see fit, in order to help you get the result you want.

Let me share an example. Let's say you want to do a wish spell. That wish spell has a list of components that includes several candles, eggshells, salt, sugar, and herbs. The way the spell is supposed to work is that you light the candles and grind up the herbs, salt, sugar and eggshells to a powder. You take the powder outside, blow it into the air and make your wish, and then go back inside and blow out the candle. It's a simple enough spell, but what if we were to modify it by getting rid of the candles, or getting rid of the components and substituting something else? Could it be possible to change the spell in the ways I've suggested?

Yes, it could be possible, because what all of those things do is provide you a specific context that you can create with them and without them. They aren't essential. What is essential is the underlying activity of the wish itself. The actions done in this spell primarily are used to focus your mind, emotions, and being in a specific way that allows you to cast the spell, but we could do a variation that serves the same purpose and doesn't necessarily rely upon all the components.

Our variation of this wish spell could go like this: Get rid of the components and candle. Take out a piece of paper and write down your wish. Then turn it into a symbol. Take the piece of paper outside with a lighter and light it on fire, inside a brazier. Once the paper is turned to ash scatter it.

Notice that we're essentially doing the same underlying working, but we've changed the expression of it. Either expression of the magical working can be done and produce results. But what I'm trying to show you is that if you understand what's actually happening with the magical working, you can take it and completely change expression of the working and still be able to perform the essential activities. And so you can modify a magical working that someone else came up with, provided you understand what they were trying to accomplish. If you understand the result, then you can develop your own process.

Let's use another example. Let's say you want to enchant a pen so that you can use it for magical workings. The original spell has you write the word activate on a piece of paper, along with a short chant, and then wrap that piece of paper around the pen. On the other side of the paper you can also write the word deactivate and another chant that deactivates the pen. Once you've wrapped the pen, you hold it to chest and say a chant and then afterwards put it on your window sill in the light of the full moon. As you can see, there's a lot of activity going on with this spell to enchant a pen.

My variation is much simpler. You pick up the pen and put it to paper and start writing, and while you're writing you channel your creative imagination into the pen. Both versions can work, but what I've done is stripped away the majority of the activities of the original spell and used the act of writing as the mechanism for charging the pen.

Now you try...

Exercise

Pick two magical workings you've done. With each one come up with an argument for simplifying the magical working (taking a minimalist approach) and an argument against simplifying the magical working. Why would or wouldn't you simplify the magical working? How would you simplify each working and how would the simplification of it make the working more efficient and optimized?

Next, try testing your simplified version and then compare it to the full magical version. What difference, if any, do you notice with the simplified version compared to the original version?

Share your answers in the Magical Experiments Facebook Group.

It's up you to determine if you're going to simplify a magical working or not. I don't think you should rule the option out, but as with anything, you ultimately have to use your own best judgement about what choice you'll make and why.

Enhancing the Magical Working

Sometimes the problem with a magical working is that something is missing, either because it's been deliberatively left out or because you recognize that the magical working could be improved on if something was added. In either case, it's possible to enhance the magical working and get better results with what you add. Before we get to that, let's consider both scenarios I've shared in depth.

Why would someone deliberately leave out essential information for a magical working? Are they playing a trick on their readers? Or is there another reason?

The truth is that information is left out for the reason that if a person attempts the magical working, it won't work and they won't harm themselves because they're missing an essential part of the puzzle. It's an understandable, if somewhat flawed reason, because while someone doing a magical working might not fully complete the working, they could still harm themselves with what they've done. I state this from personal experience because at one point I was doing some Taoist inner alchemical workings and there was key information missing, which ended up causing me to become temporarily ill. Had that information been presented in what I was working off of, I doubt I would have become ill, because it would have forced me to take my time and learn all the steps. I did eventually figure out what was missing from the work, but it seemed like a pointless power play on the part of the author.

When you come across such a situation, the author assumes that you will only be able to do the magical working if you have enough experience to recognize the missing information, but that simply isn't true. A person could still try to do the working and get bad results because key information was missing, whereas if that information was present it might actually either stop the person or really force them to take their time and understand what they were attempting to do.

In the other scenario, you might have access to all the information but see a way to enhance the actual working and improve on what it does. In that case, it really comes down to adding in your input and testing what you've changed to see if it really does produce a better result.

With both scenarios, what's important to remember is that you should take your time and test what you're doing with the working. When you learn something new, you ideally learn it in steps, making sure that you understand each step. The same principle applies to modifying a magical working, or creating one. Take your time and test everything you're doing. Record every relevant experience, and if something doesn't feel right, stop and go over everything you're doing in meticulous detail. This may seem a tedious approach to handling experimentation but taking such an approach can help you avoid problems, and it also makes sure that you really understand what you're doing.

When you decide to enhance an existing magical working, you're adding things to it that you've recognized are missing. What is it you might add to an existing magical working? You could end up adding additional correspondences or working with additional spirits. You could add additional steps that will flesh the magical working out and get the result you want. You could add tools, herbs, or other relevant components. The sky is the limit as to what you could add, however what you should keep in mind is that we want to avoid needless complexity. In other words, only add the enhancements that make sense and get you the result you want. We never want to make a magical working more complex than it needs to be.

When you decide to enhance an existing working it's useful to add enhancements only as needed. I recommend adding them one at a time so that you can see how a given enhancement changes the magical working and determine if additional enhancements are needed. The other benefit to adding an enhancement one at a time is that it will allow you to track and assess the changes that enhancement brings to the magical working. If you do all your enhancements at once you may not be able to determine how a given enhancement is interacting with the original magic working, or what is really being modified. By taking the approach I'm suggesting above you'll be able to track how your modifications effect the magical working and keep the working as optimized as possible. Let's look at a few case studies where I enhanced an existing magical working.

Case Study 1: Sphere of Art

The first example is the Sphere of Art, which is a working that R. J. Stewart shares in 3 books aptly titled *The Sphere of Art* (1, 2, and 3)[3]. One note I must make is that RJ is transparent about what details he's left out of the Sphere of Art and why he has left them out, because RJ fully recognizes that the modifications a person develops may differ from person to person.

---

[3] Available on Amazon and through RJ's website.

When I began learning the Sphere of Art, the first thing I did was just focus on learning the core working. You may look at a given working and think of enhancements you could apply to it, but I strongly recommend doing the core working first and really understanding it before making modifications. In my case, what I did was memorize each of the chants. Once I memorized the chants (which took a good few months) I started doing the core working and paying close attention to the actual experience of the ritual. By paying attention and noting observations about the experience I was able to determine what enhancements I wanted to add to the Sphere of Art working.

The central work of the Sphere of Art is focused on working with the elemental archangels of the four directions (East/Raphael/Air, South/Michael/Fire, West/Gabriel/Water, and North/Auriel/Earth). I determined that what I wanted to modify about the Sphere of Art was the following: I wanted to add an archangel for the Underworld current of energy, an archangel for Cosmic current of energy, and an archangel to tie everything together. I should note that as I was doing the Sphere of Art work, I was also doing research, which helped me recognize what could be added to the Sphere of Art. The research was specifically focused on the Quabalistic Tree of Life, and on writings by William G. Gray who had specific correspondences and archangels that fit into the sections of the Sphere that could be modified.

That research led me to make the following modifications to core work with the Sphere of Art; I added Sandalaphon for the Underworld, Metatron for the Cosmos and Suvuviel to tie everything together. I also developed chants for each of them, memorized them and then tried them out with the core Sphere of Art work. Additionally, I integrated appropriate correspondences into the chants. All of this was done as a result of the research and it was carefully tested to make sure that it made sense and enhanced the overall working. Once I tested the changes thoroughly, I then integrated them into advanced aspects of the Sphere of Art, where they meshed seamlessly.

I've continued modifying the Sphere of Art work since then, with a focus on building off the existing work with some additions of my own, which have included working with the Quabalistic Tree of Life and Planetary energies. I hope to someday do a full writeup of what I've done, but that would be its own book and dependent on getting permission from RJ Stewart, since it's based off his work. The reason I share I've done additional enhancements beyond the initial enhancements is to point out that you can potentially continue modifying a working. I do want to stress that when you do enhancements to existing magical workings, you want to base that enhancement off a combination of what your experience tells you and the research you do to back up the experiential knowledge.

None of the changes I made to the Sphere of Art were done on a whim. Rather, I made the changes after I had already done extensive work with the existing core and advanced work. I used my experiences and research to help me develop the enhancements, and tested the enhancements to see if they integrated with the sphere and deepened the existing work. If the enhancements wouldn't have worked, I would have stopped and gone back to the core work and done further research to figure out what wasn't working with the enhancements.

The Sphere of Art example I've used here is the ideal situation, where the person who originally created the working shares that they've purposively left out information and indicates what to pay attention to and provides some guidance on what to do. But what happens when you recognize that there is information from a working and yet the author/creator of the working hasn't indicated anything? Let's explore that situation with another case study below.

Case Study 2: Essence Exchange with Elementals

Some of the first books I read about magic were on the topic of elemental hermeticism and focused on working with elementals and faeries. As I worked through the exercises, one of the questions I asked myself was how I might create a closer bond with the spirits I was working with. I didn't find the answer in the books I was reading or in other books I had access to at the time, so I decided to rely upon my intuition and come up with a solution that would allow me to create that closer bond.

The solution I came up with was creating an exchange of essence, where I would use the fluids of my body, tears, saliva, blood, and cum as offerings to the faerie and elemental spirits, in exchange for some of their essence. I made this choice because of what I read in the books, which suggested that the spirits liked offerings and I felt like making an offering that was highly personal would be much more effective and powerful.

In this case there was no information that said one way or another if it was a good to make an offering of my blood, etc., and so I modified the magical working by making the choice to offer my fluids. I did all of this in the context of the specific rituals that were shared in the books I was reading. I did a ritual to each elemental king and archangel, and then made my offering and explained what I wanted. If the offering was accepted, then they agreed to exchange some of their elemental essence with me. In each case, the offering was accepted and the exchange was made.

In all fairness to the authors of the books I was working off of, they didn't indicate one way or another whether or not bodily fluids were an acceptable offering. Instead, I made the determination based off asking the question of what else I could offer. I figured that the worse that could happen was that the offering would be refused. The lesson here is that sometimes you can do a magical working and recognize that something could be changed about it, and also realize that the missing enhancement is something that no one has considered. I recognized an opportunity, where I could develop a deeper bond with the elemental spirits and chose to explore what could be done to facilitate that connection.

You can do the same. Take a look at a given magical working and ask yourself what else could be done with that working and what opportunities could be discovered if you changed the ritual and added an enhancement that the original author didn't think of or consider. Then try out the ritual with the enhancement and record what happens. You are admittedly taking a risk when you make changes that no one else has considered, but this is part of how we advance magic as a discipline, and also how we advance our own agendas. Certainly, I have benefitted from the essence exchange I've made with the elemental spirits as it's allowed me to develop some truly unique magical workings and also create deep connections with the elements that I can draw on as needed.

Case Study 3: Dzogchen Stillness Meditation

One of the meditation practices I've learned is Dzogchen Stillness Meditation. The essential focus of the meditation practice is to still your mind, emotions etc., and just be. Ideally, you aren't doing anything other than just being. You can do this in one of two ways. You can pick something to look at and focus on, just being aware of it and yourself, or you can just focus on being aware of yourself. The former version is typically used when you're just learning the stillness meditation, whereas the latter version is used when you become more experienced with the technique. With either version, if you find yourself thinking or feeling something, you want to acknowledge that thought or emotion and then let it go and focus on simply being aware.

However, something very interesting can happen when doing this stillness meditation. As you open yourself to stillness you can sometimes enter into a state of awareness where you become aware of probabilities and timelines. Now, if you're strictly sticking with the stillness meditation, you'll ignore the probabilities and timelines because they're a distraction from the stillness, but if you're like me and you're intrigued by the side effects that can occur when doing intense meditation, it can be worthwhile to explore such side effects and see what happens. And yes, if you do that you're no longer strictly doing the meditation, but the point I'm making here is that sometimes you discover happy accidents that reveal modifications on a technique in ways that the original creators wouldn't advocate for. The lesson here is to never get caught up in what other people say is or isn't possible, or what should or shouldn't be done. If you come across a side effect that might be useful, explore it and find out for sure.

In the case of the stillness meditation, when I experienced that sensation of alternate possibilities, I chose to explore it. I would meditate and then notice the probability and allow it to take over my awareness. In some cases, what it lead to was a lot of fantasizing with not much happening, but in some cases, especially when I could direct it, I would end up merging the probability with my physical reality by making it part of my body and I would find that subsequent actions would help me manifest the possibility into reality.

I ultimately didn't find the side effect of the stillness working to be very effective. More often than not, exploring the probabilities ended up being more of a fantasy trip than anything useful (and yes, I did see warnings to that effect in the instructions for the stillness meditation). But I'm glad I was open to exploring the probability side effect, because by doing that I learned why it was warned again and determined why it wasn't necessarily an effective modification of the meditation. I feel strongly that learning by doing is useful, because even though I could have heeded the advice to ignore all distractions, by really exploring what those distractions look like, it also helped me learn more about the meditation and why the modification wouldn't work. It's important to remember that not all of our enhancements will work or will be what we really want to do with the magical working.

Exercise

Take an existing magical working and determine how you could enhance it. What additions and/or changes would you make to the magical working? Why would you make those specific changes? What resources, experiences, and research do you need to do to verify and test those enhancements? Write all that information down and then do the magical working with your enhancements and note the results. Share your work in the Magical Experiments Facebook group.

Conclusion

Learning how to modify other peoples' magical workings is a good first step for learning how to create your own unique workings. When you learn how to modify someone else's working you give yourself the opportunity to analyze a given magical working and think about how it all comes together. This, in turn, can help you make significant changes to your own magical workings because you'll start seeing patterns in your work where you could improve the magical working or make tweaks that optimize what you do. You'll also start asking more questions and those questions will help you when it comes time to develop your own unique workings because you'll know what to ask, as well as how to answer those questions.

Chapter 3: How to Create Magical Workings

Now we're going to explore how to create your own magical workings and what variables you want to consider as you develop those workings. I'm going to also provide you a few examples of workings I developed and share what my overall process was for developing those workings.

If you want to develop your own magical workings, you want to consider what foundational knowledge and experiences you'll draw from to help you develop those workings. Yes, what you do will be an original working, but it will still draw on your knowledge and experience because nothing happens in a void. You may or may not draw on non-occult disciplines. As we'll see in some of my examples, I have drawn upon non-occult disciplines for the majority of my original workings, but sometimes I've drawn exclusively on different occult practices and combined them together to create my original workings.

There are two possible ways to develop an original magical working (so far as I can tell). One way involves a need to solve a problem that can't be solved by conventional solutions. The other way involves coming up with a unique approach to solving a conventional problem that provides you a better solution than the conventional solutions. Let's consider each of these ways in depth.

How to Solve a Problem with an Original Idea

Sometimes you encounter a problem that doesn't have conventional solutions that can use to solve it, or if it does have a solution, it's not a palatable solution. In such a case, you need to develop an original solution that will get you better results than the existing solutions. In such a scenario, you want to define the solution that you're aiming for and compare it to the conventional solutions that already exist. This will help you find the gap that you can use to create your own original working which allows you to solve the problem. To illustrate how this works I'm going to share a couple case studies.

Bipolar Depression

I was diagnosed with Bipolar 2 Depression, formally known as Manic Depression, when I was 18. I would have periods of time where I would feel really depressed and unable to get much done, and other periods where I was hyperactive and manic. The conventional solution was to take medication, but I didn't care for the potential side effects that would come with the medication so I decided that I had to find a different solution. But nothing I read or researched presented a solution until I came across a book, *Hands of Light*, which suggested that it might be possible to alter the physiology of the body. I did some further research and discovered the work of John Lilly, a scientist, who had used entheogens such as Ketamine to connect with the consciousness of the body, but I didn't find his solution workable because it still made me reliant upon something other than myself, which could have side effects I wouldn't want to deal with.

I needed to come up with an original solution that would allow me to heal myself of Bipolar Depression, so I took the ideas I found a step further and asked the question: would it be possible to modify the neurochemistry of the brain without relying upon external substances? Then I began to experiment with meditation, using the techniques to travel into my body and commune with it. My initial work involved changing the way my brain processed Serotonin, specifically slowing down the reuptake cycle, so that the Serotonin would stay in my brain longer. The benefit of that change was that I was able to stabilize my neurochemistry and cure myself of bipolar disorder.

In this case, I used the problem and the inefficiency of existing solutions to consider a viable solution that worked and then I tested it and came up with an alternate solution. By asking myself the question of whether or not a solution could be found that didn't involve external substances, I opened myself to considering the novelty that a person could work with the neurotransmitters and hormones of the body through magic. I drew on both occult and non-occult disciplines to come up with this solution. I used energy work and meditation techniques, but also drew on available science about the neurochemistry of the body to come up with the initial technique I used to cure myself of depression. In a later chapter, I'll share how I turned this work into a full system of magic[4].

Elemental Balancing Ritual

The elemental balancing ritual is another example of a novel solution to an existing problem. Back in 2004 I came to a realization that I needed to do some internal work on the personal issues I had in my life. I was acting these issues out and it was endangering my career at the time, but I also felt lost and unsure of how to handle my situation. The therapy resources I had access to were inadequate, and it was clear to me that I needed to find a structured and thematic approach to working through my internal issues that would help me integrate the work into my daily life in a seamless manner.

I ended up developing the elemental balancing ritual as a response to the problem. I asked myself what I could do to integrate internal work into my life and determined that what I needed to do was get my life in balance. I was already very familiar with elemental magic, and it occurred to me that I could use the elements as a contextual theme that would help me focus on the internal work, I needed to do and be relevant to my spiritual practice.

I created the elemental balancing work around the five classic elements, but I quickly realized that I wanted to expand the work beyond the classic five, so I asked a question: what is the definition of an element? The answer I came up with is something that is essential to your life and moves you. This allowed me to recognize that there could be other elements outside the classic five and I adapted the work accordingly. By opening myself to the possibility that I could work with other elements, I also enabled myself to choose what elements were actually most relevant to my needs and then start doing the work with them.

---

[4] See also the Inner Alchemy series of books, which covers how this system of magic works in detail.

I initially set up the elemental balancing ritual as a year-long ritual, which would be incorporated into the daily practice of the magician, but in recent years I've adapted it so that I could work with elements for as long as I felt drawn to work with them. For example, I worked with the element of Stillness for three years because I felt it was essential for me to understand and integrate stillness into my life. At the time of this writing, I've started my second year of work with the element of Creativity.

Doing the elemental balancing work has helped me do a continual process of internal work and allowed me to make dynamic changes in my life for the better. By setting up a year-long working with a given element, it allowed me to work on the different areas of my life where I needed helped, but it also kept the work in a spiritual context, which I found to be necessary for the work I was doing.

To do the elemental balancing ritual I used meditation techniques and daily work paired with the elemental essence I was working with. I created my own system of internal work because I felt that the ones which already existed didn't fit what I needed. What I learned from this experience is that it's perfectly acceptable to come up with one's own system of internal work to resolve a problem. And I even shared that work with other people, who have also applied it to their own lives.

Skill Sharing With Alternate Versions of Yourself

I came up with this solution because I read a comic book where the character visited alternate versions of the world. I began to wonder what it would be like to encounter an alternate version of myself. What skills and experiences would that alternate version of myself have? What would s/he be willing to exchange for access to those skills and experiences? I also reasoned that if that alternate version was already part of me, it stood to reason that we could do a skill and experience swap that would give each of us access to our respective experiences.

I know it sounds very science fiction, but I decided that I would create a technique that would allow me to access my alternate selves and make a skill swap exchange with them. The way I figured it is that if there was any basis of truth to this idea, then I would get something out of it, and if nothing else it could make a good story to write.

I used the framework of the comic book, which depicted a DNA spiral of alternate Earths as the visualization, and then I did a meditation where I visualized myself traveling to another Earth and encountering my alternate version. Then I had a conversation with my alternate self and made an agreement that we'd share experiences and skills with each other.

I found this technique worked. At the time I first devised it, I had decided to start improving my financial literacy, but I had no idea where to start. After I did the working I found myself guided to relevant materials. I also found that it was very easy to pick up the skills because the alternate version I'd shared experiences with happened to have excellent financial skills, as he made a different choice then I did.

I've done this working a few other times, and each time I've been able to share my skills with my alternate versions and get access to theirs. I've even used this technique to get glimpses of alternate versions of my life and make decisions based on what I've learned.

This particular example may seem a little fantastical because I used a comic book story as the impetus for developing the technique, but I shared it purposely to illustrate how we can develop original ideas if we are open to being inspired by what we read[5].

Wealth Magic Using Gravity and Magnetism

I came up with a wealth magic working because of a magnet toy I won at work. The magnet toy is a magnet with a bunch of metal balls on it. You can create sculptures with the metal balls. One day, on a whim, I decided to put the magnet on a metal cabinet, on the bottom of the cabinet, causing it to hang upside down. When I did this, I noticed that the metal balls stayed on the magnet, but were pulled down by gravity.

---

[5] See *Space/Time Magic* for the full explanation of how this technique works.

Seeing this happen, I began to wonder to if there was a way to create a magical working that used this magnet toy as the focus and employed the elements of gravity and magnetism as part of the working. I decided to test my idea by developing a wealth magic working that would help me get more sales for my books by attracting peoples' awareness to the ads I was running. I used the element of magnetism to enhance the attraction of the ads, and then used the element of gravity to draw in people in once they noticed the ads. I represented all of this through the magnet toy by creating the sculpture where the metal balls hang down, but, as you can see, they don't completely hang down because of the magnetism and the position they are set to in relationship to the magnet. That sculpture is the focal structure of the magical working, drawing on both elements and focusing them toward the desired result.

After I created this working, I noticed that my book sales steadily increased and that I haven't had one day where I didn't sell a book. Previous to setting up that working, I would have days where no sales occurred. At one point I did have to dismantle the magnet toy because I was moving to a new desk at my work, and around that time I noticed the sales decrease, but then start picking back up once I had rearranged the steel balls and reactivated the magnet toy.

In this case, I took what I knew about magnetism and gravity, as well as what I observed with the magnet toy, and turned it into a magical working that could be used to generate wealth. I made the magnet toy the focal point of the working because it's something I could see and manipulate. I can take the various metallic balls and massage them into the right place where they have enough magnetism pulling them up, while gravity pulls them down and they hang suspended. As I do that manipulation, I work with the elements of gravity and magnetism and attach their powers to the magnet toy, and then apply those powers to achieving the result of selling more books.

Exercise

What's a problem you have in your life that you want to solve? What conventional solutions are available to address that problem? Write those down.

Now, if those solutions didn't exist, or if they don't work for you, what original solution could you come up with that would enable you to solve that problem? Write that original solution down. What makes it different and/or better than the conventional solutions you already have access to?

Create a magical working around your original solution and implement it. Write down the results. Share your answers in the Magical Experiments Facebook group.

Improving Existing Solutions

Sometimes the conventional solutions work, but you know you could come up with something better. In such a scenario, you discover the opportunity through asking questions about how you could improve on the existing solutions. Then you create the improvement and test it to see if it works and to determine how you'll implement it.

Comic Book Sigil Method

I developed the comic book sigil method because while I found that charging and firing a single sigil worked. I thought there might be a better variation that involved multiple sigils. When I read *Understanding Comics* and the author spelled out in detail how reading comics happens (or at least his theory), I realized I had come across the perfect solution for doing multi-sigil workings.

I took his explanation for how people read comics and applied it as a magical technique. I created panels and then added sigils in them. The one modification I made was that I drew arrows between the panels to show that each sigil was connected to the other sigil.

The idea here was that the person creating the sigils would charge each of them and fire them, but set it up so that when one sigil manifested, it pulled the other sigils into reality. With this particular technique I improved on the existing explanations of how sigils work by creating a multi-sigil working using comic panels as the medium. By being open to the idea that comic book panels could be used as part of the magical working and drawing on the theory of how people read comics as part of the process for charging the sigils, I improved the existing solution of charging and firing one sigil[6].

Attention Stacking

Another modification I made to sigil work involved how sigils could be charged. I based this solution off what I learned about peoples' social media habits. Most people tend to briefly scan something in social media and move on to the next thing, which means they're giving a tiny bit of attention to whatever it is they're looking at, unless it truly captures their interest. I asked myself the question: Is there a way to harness the attention of other people, even if only for a moment, in order to use it for magical work?

Thanks to some online marketing courses I was taking, I began thinking about the possibility of using that tiny bit of attention to fuel a magical working. I figured that if you had lots

---

[6] See *Space/Time Magic Foundations* and *Space/Time Magic* for the full explanation of how this technique works.

of people seeing whatever you posted, all that collective attention could be used to charge and fire a sigil working. So, I started setting up my sigils so that when I shared them on social media, every like, comment, share, and even the brief moment of attention, could be used to charge and fire the sigil. By stacking all that interaction into the sigil, I determined that it could be harnessed to empower the magical working and fire it without the magician having to do anything else.

In this case, the improvement is on the charging mechanism of the sigil, and specifically how the sigil is charged. By taking modern concepts of marketing and applying them to magical work, I realized I could develop a new approach to charging sigils and even apply that approach to other magical workings if I wanted to. By asking the question I mentioned above, I considered the possibility that yes, there could be a way to harness that attention and then I devised it! This is why it's important to ask questions: they free your mind to consider the possibilities and from there you can turn the possibility into a reality.

Evocation Portals

The traditional approach to evocation is time consuming and involves a lot of work on the part of the magician. While I found I could do it, I also asked myself if there wasn't a better way to evoke spirits, and also a permanent means of setting up the evocation so it could be opened or closed as needed. That question prompted me to take an approach to evocation that has made the process significantly easier, while also allowing me to work with the spirits I evoke at any given moment, as needed.

The solution I came up with involves creating a painting or drawing of the sigil of the spirit I'm working with and invoking the spirit while creating the art, so that it could empower the sigil with its essence. It could then be used as an evocation portal for the spirit. After the drawing or painting is created it is hung up in the ritual room, which means the evocation portal is open. If it's taken down, the portal is closed. When the portal is open the spirit can be worked with at any time, regardless of where you are or what you're doing.

Some people might question the wisdom of setting up an evocation portal, but my approach to working with spirits is also different, based on establishing a relationship of mutual respect and symbiosis, where both the spirit and I benefit. I haven't had any ill effects occur because of this approach, and, if anything, have found that my work with the spirits is much more effective because it creates a permanent magical space that makes reality softer and easier to work with. In a future book I'll be sharing my full process for working with spirits, though you can also read about the evocation portal process in *The Magic of Art*.

In this case, I developed my own approach to evocation because the existing approach, while it works, is nonetheless time consuming. There are also ethical concerns I have about the conventional approach to evocation, and so coming up with my own solution allowed me to address those concerns and create closer relationships with the spirits that I work with. Remember that just because there is a specific way you can do a magical working, that doesn't mean you have to do it! If you find it problematic, look at how you can modify it. I took the core concept of working the sigil of a spirit and used it as the nucleus of this technique, but then developed the actual process around the sigil to come up with an easier and more efficient method of evocation.

Mansion of Memory

For our last example let's consider the classic Mansion of Memory technique, which has been used since ancient times, in one form or another, as a way of memorizing information and then sharing it with other people. The way the Mansion of Memory works is that you associate information you're memorizing with a room or an object in the mansion. Then, when you need to share that information, you visualize the mansion and the imagery you've associated with the memory to help you recall the information. It's an amazing technique.

So how could we improve on such a technique? I asked myself that very question because it occurred to me that you could do a lot more with the technique. The first thing I decided to do was approach the Mansion of Memory differently by considering that each room in the mansion would be dedicated to a specific discipline, and the information for that discipline would be stored in the chosen room. By partitioning the information of a given discipline it made it much easier to organize the information and draw on it, when desired.

The second thing I did was create an avatar of myself for each room. The avatar of a given room is assigned the responsibility of processing information about the discipline it's assigned to, and then sharing that information with me, as needed. The avatars can also collaborate with each other, which has been helpful because then they can show me how different disciplines can be combined together. This has been helpful for me in continuing to invent new magical techniques and systems.

Lately, I've also been using the Mansion of Memory to help me with my imagination. When I have lucid dreams I store the memory of them in the mansion and assign them to the avatars they are relevant to. This allows those avatars to continue working on the inspiration from the dream, and it's helped me come up with numerous fiction series that I'm starting to write.

By modifying how the Mansion of Memory works, I'm expanding what it can be used for while also evolving my own ability to process information, make connections, and put everything together. And it all came about by asking how I could improve the technique. Instead of settling for what was already there, I examined the technique and found a way to improve on it[7].

Exercise

Take an existing magical technique and ask yourself what you can do to improve it. What original idea could you come up with that would improve upon the original working and allow you to do something different with it and get at least the same results?

Once you come up with your original idea, put it to work and test it. Then share your work with us in the Magical Experiments Facebook group.

---

[7] See *Magical Identity* for the full explanation of how this process works.

Conclusion

What I've tried to do with this chapter is show how I develop original workings or improved workings. My goal here is to show you the thought process that goes into developing original workings so you can then apply that same process in the design of your own magical workings. If you understand the thought process, it becomes much easier to develop original workings because you begin to see opportunities for novelty in everything you do.

Chapter 4: How to Design and Implement Long-Term Magical Workings

Because this book is about magic by design, I decided to add this particular chapter because it is relevant to the topic, especially if you're designing your own magical workings. A long-term magical working asks for a significant commitment on your part because you'll be doing that working every day for a length of time and along the way you'll likely up modifying it, because the work changes to some degree by the nature of doing it and through the experiences you have.

Additionally, a question you want to consider is whether you want to design your own long-term magical working from scratch or work off someone else's. Before we get to that question, let's first define what characterizes a long-term magical working.

A long-term magical working is a magical working that you commit to doing each day, over a period of time, that is at the very least a month long. Why am I admittedly making a month the arbitrary least amount of time for doing a long-term magical working? Because you could do a magical working for a week and not really see significant changes, but if you do the working for a month you begin to see changes occur. In fact, with any long-term activity, magical or mundane, you typically need to commit to doing it for a month before the activity becomes a habit and before you see changes.

My long-term workings are much longer than a month. With a month, you're really just beginning to see the changes that you're creating through the working, whereas with a yearlong working, you've done it long enough that you can track the changes over an extended period of time and be able to speak to how the magical working has changed your life. The shortest long-term working I ever did was a 7-week ritual focused on the seven stages of alchemy, with each week being dedicated to a stage of alchemy. It was an interesting experience, but in general I've found that I prefer to keep the long-term workings to a minimum of a year because it really gives me time to go deep with the work.

You may wonder what the advantage is to doing a long-term working over a short-term magical working. The best way I can sum it up is that short-term workings are about the result, whereas with long-term workings, it's really about the journey, but the journey itself is the result! I do the occasional short-term working when I'm trying to get a result that I need sooner rather than later, but I prefer long-term workings because I find them to be much more effective. When you do a long-term working, you're doing it every day, and that repetition brings its own power with it. A long-term working makes reality softer, easier to manipulate, because you're repeatedly doing the working and it creates a gradual momentum that overcomes any resistance and makes the desired outcome inevitable. It should be no surprise that when I switched over to doing long-term magical workings I also found that I needed to do short-term workings less and less, because what the long-term magical working brought to my life was a fundamental alignment with the experiences I needed to have in order manifest the results I wanted.

For many magicians that will seem to go counter to how magic ought to work. They want results now, but even with a short-term working, you still need to factor in time for that result to manifest. The advantage a long-term working has over a short-term working is time and reiteration of the magical work. By being patient and doing the work over and over again you build up the momentum, and at some point, it just takes over and everything becomes much easier. In contrast, with a short-term working you're doing a lot of heavy lifting to get that result. Short-term workings can and do work, but when I compare the amount of work and effort I put into the short-term workings versus the long-term workings, I find that long-term workings take less work and are more effective because the work gets easier and easier as you continually do it again and again. The experiences you have as a result of the long-term working serve to strengthen what you're doing and increase your momentum even further.

Now, all this must sound good, but do you know why most magicians don't do long-term workings? They're impatient. They want to get results now. They want to cut corners and let's face it, magic, as it is typically written about and shared, is all about getting the result. We live in a fast paced world where people are impatient to get the result. That works if you're doing short-term workings, but long-term magical work requires that you cultivate patience and focus on doing the work without necessarily getting immediate gratification. It requires you to pay close attention to the experience itself so that you can use it to measure what you're doing. Yet, what I find fascinating about long-term magical workings, is that if you stick with them you see on-going change happen in your life that can be very dynamic and works in your favor. Continual persistent action will always be more powerful than one-off actions, because you turn the momentum of the universe itself into an ally that supports the manifestation of your work. With all that said, let's assume that you are interested in doing long-term magical workings. Let's answer the question I posed above about whether you should design your own long-term magical working from scratch or use someone else's long-term working.

Designing Your Own Working versus Using an Existing Working

I've created my own long-term workings and I've also used other peoples' long-term workings (though inevitably I've modified them). If you decide to design your own long-term magical working you'll be doing it from scratch, which means you'll have to figure out all the moving parts of the working and then put it all together. You'll also be refining that working as you continue to work with it and figure out what works or doesn't work.

If you choose to use someone else's long-term working, you'll have the benefit of working off the existing work that's been done. You'll have their instructions, information, etc., to use as you develop the long-term working. At the same time, you'll be working off their specific model or approach and you may find that you need to modify it in order to accommodate your specific needs. I'll be the first to tell you that it's perfectly acceptable to modify someone else's magical working (it is, after all, part of what this book is about).

I've purposely designed my own long-term workings so that anyone can take them and modify them as needed, because I recognized that what works for me may not work for someone else. For instance, the elemental balancing ritual has a basic structure to it, but beyond that it's entirely up to you as to how you'll work with the element you're working with. In fact, as I'll share below, I've changed how I've done the long-term work for the elemental balancing ritual a few times based on the element and other work I was doing at the time. What hasn't changed though, is the focus of the work and daily commitment to doing it.

How to Design a Long-Term Working

Whether you decide to create your own long-term magical working or work off someone else's long-term magical working, you still want to put some thought into the overall design of the magical working as well as how you'll implement it in your life. We'll cover the second part below this section, but let's focus first on the design aspect of developing a long-term magical working.

There are three scenarios to consider when you decide to design a long-term magical working. **The first scenario is**: When I design a long-term magical working, I think about what the overall purpose of the working will be and use that to define what should actually go into the magical working. **The second scenario is**: When I modify someone else's long-term magical working, I make sure that the modifications line up with the original purpose of the working unless I've decided to change that too. **The third scenario is**: If I change the purpose of a long-term working that someone else has developed, then one thing I need to determine is if the processes in that working will line up with the new purpose. Depending on what you are doing, you'll want to consider which of these scenarios applies to your situation.

Scenario 1: Designing Your Own Long-Term Magical Working

If you're design a long-term magical working from scratch, then you want to define the purpose of the working. The purpose is subtly different from a result, because a purpose is an on-going reason or call for action that defines the need for doing the long-term working. As such, the obtainment of a result may not conclude the long-term working but may indicate whether or not you're on the right path or if you need to make adjustments to what you're doing. As such, we don't strictly use the results alone to define the long-term magical working, but rather we treat them as an extension of the working that informs us as to whether or not we're on track.

What is your purpose for doing a long-term working? What are you looking for from that working, and how it will allow you to design your life? I see any long-term magical working as a commitment to not just work with a specific magical ritual for the long haul, but to also accept responsibility for designing your life around that ritual, allowing that ritual to transform your life in a very specific way. When I designed the elemental balancing ritual, the purpose of that ritual was to help me integrate internal work into my life in a meaningful way that helped me become a healthier person for myself and the people in my life. This is still an on-going purpose in my life and likely will be until the day I die.

This brings me to another point. You could do long-term magical workings that last for the entirety of your lifetime. There doesn't have to be a specific end date unless you want there to be, or unless you want there to be a conclusive ending. In the case of the elemental balancing ritual, I don't think there will be a conclusive ending until the day I die because the purpose I've used to define the long-term working is a lifelong purpose. There will always be internal work to do in order to help me become a healthier person, because there will always be opportunities where I can learn something about myself and how I interact with the world.

You might wonder then what the point is of doing a long-term working if there's no end in sight, and the point is that the purpose defines the work, but also defines you. My choice to continually do internal work to balance myself and my interactions with the world benefits me and the people in my life every day because I'm allowing the magic to work through me.

This provides me the opportunities to change in accordance with the realizations I have as a result of doing the work. It is worthwhile to remember that with long-term workings it truly is the journey itself which defines the work and ourselves as well.

Once you've defined the purpose of your long-term magical work, you need to define the form that allows you to express that purpose. The form is the actual daily work you'll do each day to manifest that purpose in your life. In the case of the elemental balancing ritual, I determined there should be a basic form used universally to dedicate one's self to the element they were going to work with for a year (or more). The actual daily work itself could vary according to the individual preferences of the practitioner, with the exception that it needs to be daily work to truly be effective. With your own long-term magical workings, you may want to stick with a specific daily practice, and you can certainly do that. Or you can change the daily practice, as long as the practice is still relevant to the purpose you're working with.

For the elemental balancing ritual, the initial practice is a dedication to the element you're working with for a year, and what I've typically done is created a painting or done some other type of magical working that switches the element I was working with to the new element I'll work with. Then comes the daily practice. When I first created the ritual I decided the daily practice should be the Taoist Water Breathing Meditation, because it's an ideal meditation technique to use for internal work and meshes well with elemental energies. I've continued using that meditation, but I've also switched up the daily practice as needed. For example, when I worked with the element of movement I incorporated some moving meditations into my daily work. When I worked with the element of Stillness I used the Dzogchen Stillness Meditation, and of late I've been using the Sphere of Art for my work with creativity (though as we'll see later, there's a bit more going on, because I'm combining two long term workings together). As you can see, the daily practice has morphed over time to fit the context of the elemental balancing ritual, but even when the daily work has changed, the underlying purpose has not. It's still the same purpose informing the work, it's just that the form has changed.

And there's no reason you can't do the same with your own long-term workings.

When you decide what form the long-term working will take you need to develop the actual processes for the long-term working. In some cases, it may mean simply using an existing technique that fits with the overall purpose of the working, but, in other cases, you might need to do some extra work. For instance, if you're using a chant with a long-term working you'll want to write the chant out and test it to make sure it fits and connects with the forces it's calling forth. You'll then need to memorize it. You might also need to do some research and explore or create correspondences. Regardless of what process you use and/or develop, you want to make sure they align with the purpose of the working and support you in doing it.

Scenario 2: Modifying Someone Else's Long-Term Working

You might choose to use a long-term working that someone else has devised, but also recognize that you need to make some modifications in order to apply the working to you. There's nothing wrong with doing that, because contrary to popular belief, magic isn't a one size fits all endeavor. Unfortunately, it's treated that way by many people who seem to gasp in horror at the idea of modifying a magical working. The truth is that though magic is a very personal activity in some ways, there's no reason not to modify a magical working if, in fact, doing so will make it work more effectively for you.

The first question to consider when choosing to modify someone else's long-term magical working is if the modification is aligned to the purpose of the work or the form of the working. If it's for changing the purpose, see scenario 3 below. If it's the form that you're changing you may have some flexibility, but another consideration that needs to be factored is whether changing the form will, in fact, impact the purpose of the work.

For the sake of argument, let's assume that you don't want to change the purpose of the work but you want to modify it because the way the long-term working is set up doesn't quite work for you. The question comes down to what you'll change. For example, let's say you were going to do my elemental balancing ritual but you decided that the Water Breathing Meditation wasn't going to work for you. You would need to come up with some type of internal practice that you could do daily that would help you work with the element. You could do a few different options, including daily Tarot cards readings to the element or doing cord work while contemplating the element, or creating a drawing/painting a day for the element. Those are just a few examples of something you could change that would still allow you to connect to the primary purpose of the long-term work but using practices that personally speak to you.

I modified the Sphere of Art working that RJ Stewart wrote about because I felt like it could be expanded upon and, as I mentioned earlier in the book, RJ was very open about the fact that it could be modified. I've already shared what I did earlier with the core work, wherein I added additional chants and correspondences, as well as worked with three additional archangels. These modifications didn't change the purpose behind the work, but rather helped to further catalyze and clarify it for me. With that said, the modifications are just that. Someone else familiar with the Sphere of Art could come up with completely different modifications that would also make sense and be appropriate in context to that person's work with the Sphere of Art. I also think that if the modifications weren't appropriate then they wouldn't work with the Sphere, because the guiding forces would make it very apparent that there was incompatibility.

Scenario 3: Changing the Purpose of a Long-Term Working

I don't recommend changing the purpose of a long-term working. You're better off either devising a long-term working of your own or finding a different long-term working. And in some cases, you may encounter a lot of resistance to changing the purpose of a long-term working. I wouldn't dream of trying to change the purpose of the Sphere of Art working because I would be running smack into the archangels, who have a very specific function in mind for the Sphere. Trying to change the purpose of the Sphere would take away from the work.

The additional issue you must deal is whether the processes that are part of the long-term work will still continue to work if the purpose of the working is changed. In some cases, they might still work, but I think you'd basically have to reinvent everything you're doing. A better approach would be to take the basic framework of a long-term working and apply it to your own long-term working. For instance, instead of changing the purpose of the elemental balancing ritual, you could take the basic framework and use it as inspiration for your own long-term working. You wouldn't copy everything I did, but you could use it to help you figure out what you would need to do to design your own working.

I strongly urge you not to modify the underlying purpose of a long-term working. The reason I included this scenario is because it is a potential scenario and I believe in covering all the bases, including recommending what not to do.

How to Implement a Long-Term Working

Once you've decided what long-term working to do you need to make a commitment. A long-term working isn't something you can slack on or take time off from. Your decision to do it means taking on daily work that you're doing to transform your life. I recommend doing an initial dedication ritual where the focus is on establishing that you will do this work every day. The dedication ritual can be the actual daily work you'll do, or it can be something else, but it should be something that ties into the work.

With the elemental balancing ritual I do an opening ritual to the element I'm working with, wherein I usually create a piece of art that is dedicated to the element. After that though, it's just a matter of doing the daily work, every day, in whatever form it is that you've decided to do it. Your hardest challenge will be doing the work on the days where it feels boring or where nothing has happened for a while, but that's when you need to stick with it the most, because that's when the work is seeding itself into your being, preparing you for the realizations and synchronizations you will inevitably have. What you must remember about doing daily work is that you are building momentum, and so during those times when the work seems slow or nothing is happen there is stuff happening, but it's happening below the surface. Stick with the work and allow it to work through you, and you will have the experiences along the way, BUT do not crave those experiences. The point of doing any of this work is that you simply you do it and allow it to work through you. Given enough time you'll have the experiences that are necessary to advance you in the work, but if you go into this daily work every day with expectations about results, you'll be disappointed more often than not because there will be days where nothing *seems* to happen (even though something *is* happening). Let go of the expectation and you'll stick with the work, allowing it to truly transform your life.

Something else you need to consider is the preparatory work you may need to do in order to prepare to do the long-term magical working. In the case of the elemental balancing ritual, there is very little preparatory work that needs to be done. You simply choose an element, do a dedication working, and then work with that element using your chosen technique each day. In contrast, to even begin working with the Sphere of Art you need to memorize the chants, and this is not a task that is done within a week or a month. It took me six months to memorize all the chants for the core working, and an additional three months to memorize the chants I created with my modifications. Sadly, most people will not make that choice to prepare for the work they'll do, because they won't consider a simple fact: the very act of memorization is an act of dedication that also attunes you to the work you'll be doing and the spirits you'll be working with. Just by memorizing the Sphere of Art chants, I already started doing the daily work and began working with the spirits.

There's a hidden benefit of memorizing the chants, as well. By memorizing them, you gradually attune yourself to the work you're doing and add it on, while also allowing yourself to process and get used to what you're working with. When you memorize a chant you are making a space for it in the essence of your being, so that when you're ready to speak it you can call forth from the innermost parts of yourself the connection you've already established with the powers you work with.

Once you've done the preparatory work then you do the daily work each day. Keep track of any experiences you have and otherwise do the work. And as best as possible, try not to skip doing the work. There will be occasions where you might need to, but, depending on how the long-term magical working is set up, you might need to start over. For example, there's a sequence in the Sphere of Art which requires that you do the work every day for a specific period of time while charging and working with specific materials. If you miss a day of that work you need to start the entire sequence over again. Other long-term workings may have similar requirements.

One way to address that requirement is to create a shortened form of the daily work you would be doing. For example, my shortened form of the Sphere of Art leaves some of the chants out, but still allows me to access the sphere. However, this is NOT a shortcut! I only developed the short form after already having worked with the Sphere for a year until I verified with the spirits that it was acceptable to come up with a short form. Even then, I still can only use it under the specific circumstance of not having enough time to do the full ritual, and the expectation is that I'll resume the full ritual as soon as possible. Remember that the point of doing this work isn't to short cut it, but rather to give yourself over to the experience so that it can speak through you. The occasional short form is acceptable, especially if you're in the midst of work you'd otherwise have to start over but doing it every day will only hurt your connection to the work and the efficacy of the experience. Only employ it as needed.

One final consideration needs to be addressed. While it's true you are doing the daily work, so too are the spirits you're working with. What you are creating and maintaining is a symbiotic relationship with them, and you will find that as you do this work your connection will deepen. However, that deepening connection brings its own responsibilities with it. For example, I could not have come up with that short version of the Sphere chants without the spirits signing off on it, because those chants are how I connect with them. If they weren't in agreement with what I was doing, then the shortened version wouldn't have been developed.

What must also be remembered with any long-term magical working is that the transformation isn't just about you, but also about your connection with the world and what you do with that connection. We don't live in a vacuum, and what long-term workings can teach us is the simple realization that the work we do impacts much more than ourselves, especially when we see it spread out over an extended period of time. We get to see the work unfold in our lives and the lives of people around us, and that provides us a perspective about our journey that may otherwise be missing when all that is engaged in is momentary work.

Combining Long-Term Workings

Another scenario we should consider is whether or not you can combine two or more long-term workings together. My answer to this scenario is a cautious, yes, with some caveats. You can potentially combine two long-term workings together, but if you take that route you need to determine if the purposes of the respective long-term workings can sync together. If they can't then don't combine them, because you'll be working at odds with yourself.

If they do sync together, you still need to consider whether the actual practices will also sync together. If the daily work you're doing for one long-term working doesn't mesh with the other long-term working, despite the purposes aligning, you either must modify the actual daily work or make the decision to keep the two workings separate. Assuming the practices align, then you can integrate the long-term workings into each other.

For example, I've integrated the Sphere of Art work into my elemental balancing ritual because the purposes of both works align, and because the Sphere of Art makes for an excellent daily practice to do in conjunction with the element I'm working with. Even so, I was very cautious about integrating the two long term workings together because I knew there needed to be a fit. The reason they fit is because the purpose of both workings is to transform the practitioner through dedicated internal work with the spiritual forces the practitioner is working with. It also helps that I chose to work with the same spiritual forces in the elemental balancing ritual that one works with in the Sphere of Art. If that hadn't been the case, I wouldn't have tried to apply the two together.

Exercises

What type of long-term magical working could you create for yourself or take on? What does the purpose of that working need to be? What specific techniques will you use to help you execute the long-term working?

Are you willing to dedicate yourself to doing the work over an extended period, every day?

Share your answers in the Magical Experiments Facebook group.

Conclusion

Designing any magical working requires some consideration and thought but designing and implementing a long-term magical working requires a level of dedication on your part that you must be sure you can commit. Long-term magical work isn't just for anyone, because doing it will change your life and not always in ways that you can anticipate or even want. And it will have an impact on the people around you, because the changes you take on will also change your relationships.

However, I think it's worth all the changes you go through. The long-term magical workings I've done have transformed my life in ways that I consider to be positive in the long-term. Sometimes the short-term changes were hard, but when I look back at them I see them as necessary growing pains that I had to go through to become the person I am continually becoming. I have become a healthier person because of the work, and I will continue to do long-term magical workings for the rest of my life.

If you decide to do a long-term magical working, it's important to know that it's your responsibility to follow through on the work and to also accept that there will be changes. There's no such thing as a magical working that doesn't change you, but long-term workings are particularly profound, and, as such, the work should not be entered into lightly.

Chapter 5: How to Create a Magical System around Your Magical Work

A magical system is a collection of magical processes that are collected together to help you achieve specific results or accomplish specific purposes[8]. I've created a few magical systems over the years and the main reason I've created each of them is because there is a gap that the system addresses. For example, my system of magic for working with the neurotransmitters and microbiota of the body came about because of the initial work I did with curing my Bipolar 2 Depression Disorder. After I got that result, I became curious about what else could be done with the physiology of the body, and as I continued to research the available techniques and processes I realized there wasn't a system of magic that specifically addressed what I wanted to do. So I decided to create one[9].

Finding the gap, which I discussed earlier in the book, is what will initially help you to not only create an original magical working (or modify an existing one), but also help you decide if you need to create a magical system of your own. You may find that creating a specific magical working for the situation isn't enough, either because there is a need for additional work or because you're insatiably curious and want to see what else could be developed around that magical working.

In the case of the Inner Alchemy of Life system, I discovered that while there was some work that hinted at what could be done with the physiology of the body, there was nothing that ties everything together, let alone anything which addressed a way to work with the life that exists within our bodies. So I developed the Inner Alchemy of Life system to

---

[8] My book *Pop Culture Magic Systems* describes how to create a magical system and is recommended if you find this chapter of interest to your own work. While I describe it in terms of pop culture, the underlying concepts can be applied to any system of magic you would want to create.

[9] See Inner Alchemy of Life for the system I created and the explanation behind it.

address that gap. The work to develop the system took place over the course of a decade and was initially done by myself. However, because I like to test what I create, I did end up having other people test the system and provide feedback, which allowed me to create a finalized form of the system that anyone can use.

That was my end goal for the system of magic I created, but it may not be yours, and that's ok. You can create a system of magic that is self-contained, or one that you share with a specific group of people, or one that is available to anyone who is inclined to do the work, but regardless of who you create the system for, it'll be done to address that gap and fix something that currently can't be fixed through more conventional means.

Let's explore what ought to go into a system of magic, so that if you decide to develop one you can start creating it. Keep in mind that what I'm presenting here is a high level overview of what you would do.

What Purpose Will Your Magical System Fulfill?

If you're going to create a magical system, the first question you'll want to consider is what purpose will your magic system fulfill? In this sense, a magical system is similar to a long-term magical working because what defines it from an overarching perspective is the purpose of the system. In contrast to a long-term magical working, the purpose of a magical system is used to define the general purpose of all the magical workings done in that system.

Here are a couple of examples of magical system purposes. The purpose of my Space/Time Magic system is to learn how to apply the elements of space and time to magical working to get better results. That purpose defines everything I do with the Space/Time Magic system, which is helpful in terms of determining what magical workings apply to that system.

Another example of a magical system purpose is the purpose behind the Process of Magic system: The purpose is to understand how and why magic works in order to get better and consistent results. Again, everything done in that system needs to fit that purpose. I could share a few more, but I hope you get the picture. Defining the purpose of the magical system will help you clarify what goes into that magical system and what should stay out of it. Not every one of my magical workings fits in a given system, and by having that clarity of what fits into the system and what doesn't allows me to develop magical workings with appropriate criteria, and also enables me to evaluate them with the same criteria.

The purpose also speaks to the gap that the magical system is addressing. In the case of the Space/Time Magic System, the gap is a lack of a coherent system of magic for working with space/time. It's true that other people than me have developed space/time magic workings, but no one else has developed a magical system explicitly focused on space/time magic (or if they have, they aren't writing about it). What this should illustrate is that a singular magical working does not a system make. Thus, we can also say that a magical system is a collection of magical workings explicitly focused on fulfilling the purpose. I'd add an additional optional caveat and say that a living system of magic is one where on-going research and development of magical techniques is happening.

In the case of the process of magic system, the gap being addressed is the lack of a focused explanation of how and why magic works. The system has been developed to address that gap and also make the overall discipline of magic more accessible and easier to learn. One of the sub-purposes of this system is that I seek to strip away the needless complexity and unnecessary jargon of esotericism, which so many occultists are in love with because of the image factor. You can have sub-purposes which further clarify the overall purpose and help keep you on task with what you're seeking to accomplish with the magical system you're working in.

Exercise

If you want to create a magical system, what is the purpose of that magical system? How does that purpose define the focus of the magical workings that you're doing? Are there sub-purposes in your system of magic, and how do they clarify and enhance the overall purpose?

Write your answers down and share them in the Magical Experiments Facebook group.

What Principles of Magic Will You Draw On?

Once you've defined the purpose of your magical system, you'll want to consider what the principles of magic you want to apply to the system of magic. You don't need to have them defined from day 1 of your magical system, but you should give some thought to them. I am continually developing and testing principles of magic that I develop for each of my systems. I don't treat them as hard and fast rules, because there may be experiences that indicate that a principle needs revision, or even that it might be wrong. I treat principles as descriptors of how the workings in the system of magic ought to work, but I also fall back on the most important principle you can ever learn: challenge what you know to discover what you can learn! As such, a magic principle ought to always be open to revision.

A principle of magic can be used in multiple systems of magic. For example, the principles of magic that I developed for the Process of Magic apply universally to my other systems of magic, but you can also have specific principles for specific systems of magic. The Inner Alchemy of Life system of magic has a principle that emphasizes the importance of using the experience itself to communicate with the spirits of the body. The Space/Time Magic system has several probability principles that apply to how space and time are used to create results. These principles actually could be applied universally, as well, but they can be useful to also consider the specific context of the principles for the system itself.

So, how you do describe and/or define the principles of magic that you'll use? You can draw on someone else's principles of magic, if you're not sure, as a good starting place[10]. But I'd also suggest taking a look at your magical workings. How do they work? What are the practices you do across the board with your workings? What are the underlying actions that

---

[10] See The Process of Magic or Isaac Bonewitz's Real Magic for examples of principles of magic.

make those practices work? Answering those questions can help you determine if you have a principle of magic.

For instance, my principle of connection is informed by the various magical workings I've done including invocation, evocation, enchantments, etc., because I've noticed how connection plays a role in making magic work. My recognition of connection and the actions that seem to go along with the principle has helped me create that principle and use it to describe how magic ought to work. Of course, I'm open to revising that principle should I come across experiences that indicate something I've missed about connection, but until that happens I'll use the principle to explain what ought to be happening.

Having principles of magic in your system provides the benefit of troubleshooting your magic, because if you know you're a specific principle but the magic working isn't happening the way the principle describes you can use that principle to troubleshoot the issue and either determine that the principle needs to be revised, or that you missed something essential to making the principle work[11].

I recommend that as you develop the principles of magic for your system, keep a cheat sheet that describes what each principle is and how it ought to work. Having this cheat sheet to reference can help you as you design your magical workings and decide on what principles apply to the working and where they fit into the working.

What Spirits Will You Work With?

The majority of magical systems have spirits that a person can work with, if they choose to. There is the rare magical system which doesn't have spirits to work with, but for the sake of argument we'll assume that you'll be working with spirits (or archetypes or however you want to typify them). If that's the case, you'll want to decide what spirits would best fit into the system and then contact them through invocation and see if they are receptive to working with you.

---

[11] See How to Troubleshoot Magic for more details on troubleshooting magic.

You'll also need to be cautious and not just try to randomly cherry pick spirits. Aside from the fact that you may or may not be engaged in cultural appropriation if you go down that route, there's also the complication of whether or not the spirits you want to work with are all mutually compatible. If you're doing magical workings with the spirits, you want them to work with you and collaborate with each other.

The way I approach this is that I ask myself if the spirits I'd work with fit with the overall purpose of the system. If they don't, that rules them out, but if they do, then I'll ask myself if there would be any potential conflicts with the spirits that I'd want to work with, as well as what those conflicts might be. If there are no potential conflicts, then I would proceed. If there are potential conflicts I'd recommend seeing if you can find spirits that are more compatible or choosing which specific spirit you'll work with. I don't recommend asking the spirits if there's a way for them to work together, because if the conflict is there, it'll just exacerbate the situation and could make your life miserable. For example, I knew a practitioner that thought working with Kali and Morrigan was a grand idea. But it really wasn't a grand idea, because while both spirits might have similarities, the differences that were ignored were quite critical. She chose to cherry pick how she wanted to work with the spirits, but discovered that they would have none of it. Her life ending up blowing up because of the anger both spirits felt. It took some time and effort on her to make amends and taught her a valuable lesson.

Once you've determined what spirits to work with, you'll want to connect with them and see if they're amendable to working with you. If they aren't, don't try and force a fit. If they are, then explain what you want to do and make whatever agreements needs to be made to secure their help. Once you've got that you'll continue working with them, and at the point you may find that they have their own insights and perspectives to share about your system of magic. I recommend being open to what they share, as it will likely help you develop and refine your magic system further. This leads us to the next part of the system to define.

What Correspondences Will You Use?

As you work with the spirits in the system you're developing you'll find that they'll provide you valuable information that will help you flesh out your system. Among other information that will be provided, you'll end up learning about correspondences. Correspondences is information you use to show how your system connects to the various forces you work with. An example of a correspondence might be North – Earth – Auriel, where in the direction of North and Earth is connected to the archangel Auriel. Thus, when you work with Auriel, you're also working with the direction of the North and the element of Earth.

The value of correspondences is that it allows you to stack and associate specific information with specific spirits. When you work with those spirits, you're accessing that information and the power it represents through the spirit. The spirit mediates that power for you, making it accessible in a way that you can handle. If you're working with Auriel, then Auriel is mediating the power of elemental Earth and giving you access to what's safe for you to handle.

Another function of correspondences is that they indicate the sphere of influence that a spirit has access to. A spirit that has an association of wealth attributed to it may have some useful information to draw on for any wealth magic workings you want to do. The correspondences you develop will help you build your system of magic, because you'll be able to use the attributions in the magical workings you develop for that system.

What Occult Disciplines Will You Draw On?

Building a system of magic doesn't happen in a vacuum. You'll draw on your previous experiences with various occult disciplines you've learned in order to help you build that system. One question you'll want to consider is what occult disciplines you'll use in your system. For example, will you use a divination practice in your system, and, if so, what specific divination techniques will you use? If you've already connected with spirits, then you'll have already used invocation and possibly evocation techniques to work with them. And then there's practical magic techniques as well that you might draw on.

But it's not just the techniques we're looking at, but also the actual disciplines and the experiences you have with them. When I developed my Space/Time Magic system, it's fair to say that my experiences with Chaos magic, as well as ceremonial magic, played a role in how I developed that system. For that matter, my experiences with Taoist meditation practices also played a role in helping me develop the meditation techniques.

For your own system of magic you'll want to draw on your previous experiences and the existing systems you're familiar with. You don't necessarily want to copy those systems into your existing one, but at the same time you do want to look at them and ask yourself what could be applied or used as inspiration for your own system of magic.

Each system of magic I've developed has drawn on my previous experiences and the disciplines I've studied. Sometimes what I've worked with previously has even helped me determine what I don't want to work with. You can compare your system of magic to what you've studied, and it will help you identify what you want to do, but also what you don't want to do.

What Non-Occult Disciplines Will You Draw On?

One of the things which makes my systems of magic distinct from most other magical traditions and systems that people can learn from is that I draw on non-occult disciplines as well as occult disciplines to develop the system. The reason I do that is because I find that the non-occult disciplines can offer perspectives and techniques that may be relevant to your system of magic.

I've used neuroscience and biology with the Inner Alchemy of Life system, and with the Space/Time Magic system I've drawn on physics, as well as anthropological perspectives on time, to inform the development of the system. We shouldn't rule out non-occult disciplines because they don't have occult terminology. At the same time, we do need to recognize that applying those disciplines to magic still requires a specific context that ought to be considered carefully. For instance, the tendency to treat magic as a psychological phenomenon is not accurate to how magic works and has led to a diluted understanding and experience of magic. Certainly, we can apply psychology to magic, but we should do so carefully and that same advice applies to any non-occult discipline.

The way I approach the integration of non-occult disciplines into an existing or new system of magic involves using my understanding of magic as the lens by which the non-occult discipline is applied to magic. When I developed the multi-sigil technique using comic books, I based it off what I learned about how people read and process comic books. I asked myself how what I learned could be applied using an occult understanding of the concepts. You want to do the same with any non-occult disciplines you integrate in your magical work and/or system. We don't want to remake magic into a non-occult discipline. We want to apply magic to that non-occult discipline in order to come up with new magical workings.

What Tools Will You Use?

We all use magical tools. They may differ from magic system to magic system, but nonetheless we use tools of some type. The question you must ask is what tools you'll use for your magical system. It helps if we define what the tools actually are. When you think of magical tools you might think of an athame, staff, or pentacle, and that would be correct. But you might also think of candles, incense, herbs etc., as tools and that would also be correct. Additionally, you can create your own magical tools for specialized needs. I've created a number of tools over the years because there isn't a traditional equivalent to them and I needed something for the work I was doing.

What really makes something a tool of magic is that you have a specific need for it in order to help you accomplish your magical working. A tool serves to mediate the forces you are working with, helping you to connect to those forces and access them in a way that allows you to understand and use them.

Let me share an example. One of the tools I've created is the Memory Box. The Memory Box is a box of wood with a silver web painted on the inside. The Memory Box is used to access the web of Space/Time which displays space/time as a web. The vibrating strands of the web are the movements of time, while the nodes where the strands meet are the spatial identities that time creates. I developed the Memory Box as a means to access the web of Space/Time, but also to help me process the information[12].

I want to be clear that a magical tool isn't a symbol. A magical tool helps you connect to the forces that the tool embodies and mediates. The tool doesn't merely represent those forces, but instead allows direct access to them, albeit in a manner that is designed to help you work with those forces safely.

When you're developing your magical system, you'll want to consider what forces you're working with and what magical tools will best help you access those powers. You may also need to invent such tools, if they don't already exist, but that can prove to be useful for helping you develop your system further. In my development of the Memory Box and the web of Space/Time, I needed tools that could help me work with the elements of space/time in a way that hadn't been previously written about in other books on the topic. I was taking my own understanding of space/time and turning it into a magical tool that I could use to work with that understanding. You may need to do the same with your own ideas, and this is why it can be useful to not just rely upon traditional tools, but also develop your own tools.

Regardless of whether you invent a magical tool of your own or use a traditional one, you ought to be clear on what function that tool serves in your magical system and how it helps you do magical workings in your system. I recommend writing down a description of how the tools work, based on the work you've done with them. Update those descriptions as needed for your magical systems, based on the experiences you have with the tool.

I also recommend working with the tools directly, just for the purpose of getting to know them, and embody them in your own life. One of the most pivotal magical workings I did

---

[12] See Magical Identity for the full explanation of the Memory Box and the web of Space/Time

involved working directly with the traditional tools of magic and embodying them in my body, making them part of my identity. By becoming the tools, I took them into myself and it made it even easier to access the forces they represented because the magical tools showed me how to work directly with those forces. I do the same practice with the tools I invent, gradually integrating them into my identity so that I can work with the forces directly.

You may wonder what I mean by working with the tools directly, so let me share two examples. The first example is the rod or wand. The rod/wand is a traditional magical tool, typically associated with the element of fire. I meditated on the rod, allowing it to teach me about the element of fire, and then in the meditations I took the rod into myself and embodied it, letting its consciousness and identity become part of my own, which then allowed me to work with the element of fire directly because I had essentially become the tool. Now when I do magical workings that would normally involve a rod, I simply allow that identity to come through my body and use that work with the element of fire.

Likewise, I created the Memory Box to initially help me process the web of Space/Time, but I meditated with it so that I could embody that understanding of the web of Space/Time directly. This allowed me to eventually access the web without the Memory Box, because the tool has become part of my identity and I can access it through the embodied experience I brought into myself during my work with the tool.

This is admittedly a different approach to working with magical tools, which typically are externalized into a physical shape. It's useful to work with the physical tool, but I find that's just the start of your work, and if you choose to work with it exclusively for the purpose of embodying the tool you can discover some very interesting experiences that shape not only your magical system, but how you work with magic in general.

What Chants Will You Use?

I find that the medium of sound is a powerful tool in its own right, and we are blessed because we can use sound in magic. As such, I recommend using sound in the development of your system. One of the most potent ways you can use sound involves chanting. I like chanting because it's a great way to work with your correspondences and spirits while imprinting them on the internal environment of your mind and body.

You can use pre-existing chants, but if you're developing your own system of magic I recommend coming up with your own chants. What should go into those chants? It depends on what the purpose of the chant is. If you're invoking or evoking a spirit, then the chant ought to be to the spirit. I such a case, I'd recommend including relevant information in the chant that links the appropriate correspondences to the spirit.

If your chant is for a different purpose, such as an inducing an altered state of mind, I recommend keeping it simple. I've used various vowel chants, which make for an excellent way to induce an altered state of mind, because they disrupt the usual thinking a person does and brings them to a place of calmness.

Regardless of what chant you come up with you'll want to memorize that chant. By committing it to memory, you make it part of yourself and you have the additional benefit of being able to use it wherever you are. Below is an example of a chant I developed while working with the archangel Khamael:

Hail Khamael of the purifying fire
Guardian of Geburah
Martial discipline and judgement
Are your gifts to us.
You teach us discernment
While burning away the dross
And cutting the chaff
Here in this space we acknowledge you.

This is a relatively simple chant, but what it does is capture the necessary correspondences that are relevant to Khamael. It can be memorized and used to invoke Khamael. If you were to develop a similar chant, you want to keep it focused and relevant to the spirit it is for. When you say the chant, you are conditioning your internal reality to be receptive to the external reality of the spirit and create a symbiotic relationship where you can work together.

Experiential Embodiment

There is one last aspect of a system of magic that is not typically written about, but must be paid close attention to. That aspect is experiential embodiment. Throughout much of this chapter I've actually written of it, with examples of what it is. But what is experiential embodiment?

Experiential embodiment is the choice to embody the magic in yourself, to make it part of your identity, part of the flesh and spirit that makes you what you are. At the same time, experiential embodiment is the choice to open yourself to the experiences and let them speak through you, mediating the magic you work, while letting it carry you where you need to go.

One of the failings of modern magic is that so much of it is treated as an intellectual exercise. You'll hear people say that magic is in all your head and treat it as a psychological phenomenon, or try to box magic into some model that explains away some aspects of magic in favor of others. This failing has served to dilute magical theory and practice.

I prefer an experiential approach to magic, where I do the magical work and open myself to experience and embody it in my identity and body. This approach requires a certain willingness to just let go and do the magic with a faith that belies the need to theorize magic to death. Instead the focus on experience brings us closer to the mysteries of life and death, the heart of the universe, and the hidden potential that beckons us to discover who we can really be.

I write about the process of magic, which on the surface may seem like an intellectual exercise, but it is driven by observation and experience, by becoming the magic and letting it work through me. A truly effective system of magic must challenge you to transform, to take on the work and become something different as a result. Experiential embodiment is the exact opposite of the attempt of many magicians to distance themselves from magic and the results they get. Experiential embodiment recognizes that the genuine experience of magic is found in the choice to take on the identity of the work you're doing, to invite it to change you and your relationship with your results and with the universe itself.

When you create a system of magic and work with it, open yourself to the experience and let it speak to you and through you. If you do that, not only will you create a system of magic, but it, too, will also create you.

Conclusion

What I've provided in this chapter is an overview of what you need to think of when you decide to create a magical system of your own. These are the elements that I consider to be essential to creating a system of magic, but you may find there are elements I left out. I'd suggest using this overview as an initial guide to helping you create a system of magic. I've opted not to include an exercise for this chapter, because if you're going through the overview and applying it toward creating a magical system, you're already doing the work.

Not everyone will create a system of magic, but if you choose to do it, it's something you'll likely spend the rest of your life working on in, in one form or another. I'm continually working in and developing my own systems of magic, and I find it to be quite rewarding, both in terms of doing the work and exploring the questions and answers such work inevitably leads you to.

Chapter 6: Q and A

In this chapter I'm going answer questions people asked in the Magical Experiments Facebook group in relationship to this topic and share my own answers. My answers aren't the authoritative answers, but they are my perspective on the questions they asked. I would invite you to come up with your own answers, because in the end, you are the ultimate authority of your spiritual path.

Q. One thing that I would like to see is discussion on how to approach changing spell ingredients - not just "these things are all basically the same" or "these things are all for drawing wealth, so any will do" or "you can use sandalwood or frankincense to replace anything". I think I would like to know why someone chose the steps and ingredients that they did-what was the mind behind it all? Did they choose an herb because it is known for doing a certain thing, or was it because they had experience with it? Would you choose an herb or step because everyone says so, or would you think about how your own mind could be changed through something more personal? And is it okay to radically change the process because you were looking for something that created a realness for you?

A. I don't use a lot of components in my magical work, but I recognize other people do. On the rare occasion I have used components such as herbs, oils, and incenses, what I've done is researched what I'm using so I understand why it even applies to the magical working. I also research appropriate substitutes, with an eye toward making sure that those substitutes can actually stand in for what's being replaced.

While the research is helpful, I also pay close attention to the experience. If I'm using an oil, for example, I pay attention to how it makes me feel and how the smell engages me in the overall magical experience. By focusing on the experience I can let my intuition guide me about whether to continue working with that component, or if I can replace it or even stop using it. With anything I do, I ask myself what makes that component, action, etc., essential to the process, and if I can't answer that question then I start experimenting with not using that component, action, etc., to see if there is a difference in the magical work and, if so, if that difference is positive or negative.

For example, with a long-term working I'm doing I chose to forgo lighting a candle that I typically use with the working to see what would happen if the candle wasn't included. I didn't discover a significant difference with or without the candle, but I also considered that the purpose of the candle was to connect the work to the larger current that the working is part of. That ultimately informed my decision to keep lighting the candle, since that current is significant to my overall work. But choosing not to light the candle was useful for determining why I ought to care.

I never blindly follow the words of other magicians on why a working ought to be done a certain way. I'll consider their perspective, but I always weigh it against my own perspective and experience and use that to determine what I'll do and why I'll do it.

I do think it's more than okay to change the process radically to achieve a realness to your magical work. I did it with evocation and I've done it with other workings. If something you're doing doesn't feel real, but you feel like you could do it better if you changed things, then make the changes and see what happens. Your resultant experiences will teach you a lot about the magical working...and yourself.

Q. How do you decide when to do a long-term working versus a short-term working?

A. It comes down to what the purpose of the working is. In general, it seems like short-term workings are oriented toward getting specific results, while long-term workings are focused on a process of transformation that occurs throughout the entirety of the working. I typically do short-term workings when I want to get a specific result or solve a problem. I do long-term workings to fulfill a specific purpose and I'm less concerned about the results, because the focus of the long-term work is on the journey, as opposed to a specific result.

Q. What "structural frame" do you put around magical workings? What have you found more/less useful/durable, etc.? By structural containers I mean that I've used webs, weaving, wells (containers of energy), and motion sensors (triggered by x).

A. My structural frame is the process of magic. I don't rely upon spells, webs, weavings etc., unless they're useful as a metaphor to describe the process. The reason I use process as my structural frame is that a process is much more encompassing than any other descriptor I've found. It's also organic, in the sense that it can be changed and often is, as one inevitably needs to adjust and adapt the magic working to the situation.

The benefit of using process as a frame is that it allows you to organize your magical workings. You have an ending (the result or transformation), a beginning (the need to do the magical working), and all the actions you take, as well as the variables that effect the magical work. The process allows you to map it all out and make changes as needed, while also letting you track everything you're doing.

Q. How do you stay coherently connected to the beginning of a long-term magical working? What helps you remember to stick to it? How do you keep up the enthusiasm to want to continue?

A. I stay connected to the beginning of a long-term working by making the beginning into an event of its own, but also remembering that the beginning is part of the continuum of the work. I mark the beginning as a special event because I'm making the choice to dedicate an extended portion of my life to the work, and I want to show that I'm ready to fully commit. I recommend doing something similar as well when you commit to a long-term magical working.

What helps me stay committed to the working is making sure that I make it part of my daily life. If it's not part of my daily life, then I'm not really engaged in the working and that's the point of doing a long-term working. Now I recognize that some people will find daily work challenging, but it doesn't necessarily need to take up a huge portion of your day. What you need to do though is commit to consistent work so that you can allow the magic to work through your life.

As for keeping up enthusiasm, what I do is remind myself that long-term work isn't about results. It's about the process and the journey. I recognize there will be days where the work isn't that exciting. I also recognize that what I'm really doing is allowing the work to become embodied and the moments of excitement will happen exactly when they need to. Long-term magic work isn't a sprint. It's a marathon.

Conclusion

At the beginning of this book I told you that I wrote this book because I was inspired by an interaction I had where an individual shared how bored they were with their magical work. What I didn't share with you was another reason I've written this book.

I want to help you find joy in your magical workings. Magic ought to bring a sense of joy to one's life. Certainly it has for me, and so that too is a reason I've written this book, because if there is no joy in your work it means you've hit a dead end. If that's the case, it's my hope that this book has helped you figure out how to get out of that dead end and find meaning in your magical work once again.

Sometimes we must walk our own paths. In fact, if you're really to be a magician, you must learn to walk your own path because no one else's path will do. I've walked my own path for most of my life, seeking my own answers, asking my own questions, and never letting anyone else tell me what I could or couldn't do with magic (or anything else for that matter). Part of that I learned by defying the orthodox, conventional wisdom of thou shalt not experiment with magic or do anything that someone else hasn't told you to do.

My hope is that you'll do the same. Afterall, if we are to be magicians we cannot stay in the shadows of those who have come before us. We must learn from them, but also challenge them. We must discover for ourselves how magic works, and that can only happen if you are willing to challenge what you know by discovering what you can learn.

Taylor Ellwood
November 2019
Portland, OR

Thank you for reading Magic by Design!

If you found *Magic By Design* helpful to you I would really appreciate it if you would write a review. Even one or two words is more helpful than you can know.

Please leave a review on Amazon, Goodreads, and Bookbub.

You finished Book 5 of the How Magic Works series and there's more on the way

I'm currently working on the next book in the How Magic Works series, The Magic of Writing. If you'd like to be notified when that book is available, please visit the magical experiments site at http://www.magicalexperiments.com/free-books and pick up a free e-book on magic, and get placed on my e-list so you can get notified when the Magic of Writing is out.

Also check out the bonus chapter in this book, which is the first chapter of *Pop Culture Magic Systems*.

About the Author

Taylor Ellwood is the author of numerous books on magic including Pop Culture Magick, Space/Time Magic, and Inner Alchemy. He is also the author of Learning How To Fly, a super hero novel about a hero who needs to go to remedial flying school. When he isn't working on his latest magical experiment or writing a book he can be found enjoying games, books, and life and the company of his amazing wife. For more information about his latest non-fiction projects, check out his site http://www.magicalexperiments.com. For more information about his latest fiction projects, please visit http://www.imagineyourreality.com

Learn How Magic Works!

Free E-books available on my website
Magicalexperiments.com

Whether you want a learn a simple 4 step process for creating a magical working, or discover how take your fandom and turn it into a spiritual practice, or learn simple breath meditations that enhance your life, or discover how to turn probabilities I have free e-books available for you that will teach you how magic works and how to get consistent results with it. Visit magicalexperiments.com/free-books and download your free e-book today!

Chapter 1: What is a pop culture magic system and why would I want to create one?

When I first started practicing pop culture magic, there were no systems available for it. My initial work was very much in a vacuum in one sense because while there were systems of magic and traditions of magic already in existence, it wasn't necessarily easy or desirable to map pop culture magic to those systems. At the same time, in order for pop culture magic to have any depth, developing a system was essential.

I developed my first system of pop culture magic with Storm Constantine; the Dehara system, which is based off the *Wraeththu* series written by Storm. She, myself, and a few other people worked in tandem to develop a workable system of magic that drew on pre-existing systems and traditions of magic, but also had original content that was specific to the *Wraeththu* series and to the actual magic we developed. We shared our initial results in *Grimoire Kaimana*, and a decade later we shared further developments in the system via *Grimoire Ulani* and *Grimoire Nahir-Nuri*.

Why did it take a decade for us to share further work with the pop culture magic system we developed?

There are a couple answers to that question. First we got busy with our own respective projects, and second in some ways the system itself had to mature and be worked with. Once that work had been, we could go deeper and see what else came about as a result.

I don't share that with you to discourage you from developing your own pop culture magic systems, but rather because developing such a system isn't something done in a day, or a year. In fact you never really stop developing a system of magic. Ideally your system changes over time, and in fact for your system to become viable (i.e. to be something more than just a one person show) it ultimately has to change, in a way that can actually be very challenging for the originator of the system.

The challenge is this: At some point, if you want your system of magic to be worked with by other people, you have to surrender control of that system and recognize that people will make changes to it that you may not always agree with or even like, but yet may be needed in order for that system to have relevance to those people. Whew! That was a mouthful to write, but it's true.

A system of magic (and tradition for that matter) is only relevant if people practice it. Unfortunately many magicians and Pagans have a tendency to treat their systems and traditions as holy cows that should never be poked, prodded, critiqued or experimented with. The problem with that tendency is that it makes those systems and traditions less and less relevant because they don't change.

Now, in their defense, not all change is good. Just accepting any change can be as big a problem as accepting no change. If a system or tradition is going to be relevant, desired changes need to be examined, critiqued and vetted. In other words, yes a system or tradition of magic must adapt to the times and needs of the people practicing it in order to be relevant, but the adaptations need to be critically examined to make sure they really support and continue the system or tradition.

System and Tradition are not one and the same

As you've may have noticed I've been using the words "system" and "tradition" as I've been writing this first chapter. After this chapter we will only be using the word system, but I purposely included the word tradition because I want to make several important points about the words "system" and "tradition". These points need to be made in order for us to fully appreciate what we're actually developing in this book.

The first point is this: The words "system" and "tradition" are not interchangeable words and should not be treated as such. Unfortunately they sometimes are treated as interchangeable words that mean the same thing. They don't mean the same thing. We need to have clarity around these words so that we understand what we're doing with this book and whatever system you develop as a result of reading it[13].

A system of magic is a series of processes and techniques developed by a magician for the purposes of connecting with the divine (in whatever form the divine shows up) and for turning possibilities into reality. The system is used to organize these processes and techniques so that they can be shared with other people, either through books (such as this one) or through classes or in-person transmission.

A Tradition of magic is also a series of processes and techniques (done for the same reasons mentioned in the above definition), but those processes and techniques have been developed by multiple generations of magical practitioners and passed down as part of a spiritual lineage. A Tradition of magic has Inner Contacts (spiritual ancestors) who help to mediate the tradition and spiritual forces associated with the tradition.

The difference then is this: A Tradition of magic has been around for at least a few generations, while a system of magic is something which has been developed in the present or recent past. At the time of this writing there are no pop culture traditions of magic, but there could be someday.

Now the definitions I've presented here are very technical definitions of the words "system" and "tradition" when used in context to magic. I've opted for a technical definition of both words because it makes it easier for us to focus on actually doing the work of creating and developing a pop culture system of magic.

The second point is this: Your system of magic could become a tradition of magic but you will likely not be alive when that happens or if you are alive, it will be much further down the

---

[13] An excellent book to read about the power of definitions is Defining Reality by Edward Schiappa.

line than now. I write that because I want you to understand that what you are creating is a system of magic as opposed to a Tradition of magic. Your system could evolve into a tradition of magic, but if it does it will take a while.

Can my system of magic just be for me?

You might wonder if you can develop a system of magic that is just for you. And the answer is yes you can. People do it all the time. However, such a system is self-contained and as a result will go away when you either die or stop practicing it. If it isn't shared, the system won't be viable for anyone else other than you. And that's fine if that is what you want. You can take what you learn in this book and create your own system of magic without ever sharing it with other people.

In fact, I'd argue that one of the challenges for a pop culture system of magic is actually finding people interested in practicing it. We all have our individual interests in pop culture and so developing a pop culture system of magic for other people can be challenging. The reason Storm and I were able to pull it off is because she had a fan base that already practiced magic and was intrigued by the idea of doing magical work with the characters of the *Wraeththu* series. Yet don't let that stop you from sharing your system of pop culture magic with other people, because you may find they are interested in practicing it.

What is pop culture?

If you've read *Pop Culture Magick* and/or *Pop Culture Magic 2.0*, you already know the answer to this question. For those of you who haven't read those books, I'll provide a concise definition AND recommend you pick up both books, as the material in those books will help out immensely with this book.

Pop culture is the contemporary culture of the present. In other words, its culture that is relevant to the people living now. What makes pop culture relevant are the people who reference it and use it in their lives. For example if you watch a T.V. show, that show is a relevant piece of pop culture for you. Pop culture isn't necessarily popular to everyone, but it is meaningful to you and because it is meaningful you can work with it magically.

For the purposes of this book, what you're learning is much more than just working with pop culture magically. You're learning how to create a pop culture magic system that can be worked with by you and other people over an extended period of time.

What is a pop culture system of magic?

A pop culture system of magic is a system of process and techniques constructed around a specific expression of pop culture, which also utilizes the principles of magic. It may or may not include working with pop culture spirits and deities. The pop culture system of magic is devised in order to provide structure and depth to your magic work with the specific pop culture you've chosen to work with. The reason you put the system together is because you've committed to working with that specific experience of pop culture. The system provides the necessary organization and rigor needed to make the pop culture magic more than just a short term working done to solve a problem. You're developing a spiritual path that allows you to deepen you connection to the pop culture you work with, through the magic you practice.

Think of a system of magic as a map. It describes how magic ought to work and what you need to do in order to make it work. Essentially what we're creating here is your map for your pop culture magic.

Again this is a very technical definition and I've purposely chosen to be very technical because ultimately what I want is for you to figure out what a pop culture magic system looks like. This book is meant to be a guide and provide some insights, but you ultimately have to do the heavy lifting in order to create your pop culture magic system.

Where does pop culture Paganism fit into creating a pop culture magic system?

There are some people who don't practice magic and primarily consider themselves to be pop culture Pagans. This book may still be useful to you in terms of considering some of the details of creating a pop culture Pagan system you can work with. That said, this book is primarily about creating a pop culture magic system, so I assume that the majority of people reading this book do practice magic and consider it to be an integral part of their spiritual practice.

Can I create a pop culture magic system if I don't have a lot of experience?

If you don't have a lot of experience practicing magic, I don't recommend trying to develop a pop culture system of magic, because the honest truth is you don't have the experience or knowledge of magic that you really need to have in order to put together such a system. I can fully appreciate the desire to create your own system of magic, but you first need to understand how magic works and that doesn't happen overnight. Additionally you need to develop the necessary level of discernment and critical thinking that is essential to avoid putting yourself into a situation where you are deluding yourself about your experiences.

I also think you need to spend time just learning to work with pop culture magic. You might have a favorite pop culture you want to develop into a system, but I recommend working with a couple other pop cultures that you like, but you aren't as heavily into so that you can get some experience working with pop culture magic. That experience, in turn, will help you immensely when you are ready to develop a pop culture system of magic.

A pop culture system of magic is a commitment and it won't always be fun. Sometimes, in the development of that system, you're going to have experiences that will call on you to grow. You want to already have some of those experiences before you start developing your pop culture system of magic.

Why is spiritual discernment and critical thinking so important?

Spiritual discernment and critical thinking play an important role in developing *any* system of magic. Spiritual discernment is what you use to check and verify that the spirits you are working with are really spirits and the information they provide you is accurate. In pop culture magic, this is especially important because sometimes people get caught up in wishful thinking. They really want to have a connection with a pop culture character and they want that connection to occur in a specific context (usually romantic or sexual)[14]. What they are doing is ascribing their own needs and desires onto the character. They practice magic, but they don't use spiritual discernment and as a result they end up in a situation where they've deluded themselves.

Critical thinking is also essential because it helps you to ask the necessary questions such as, "Why am I drawn to work with this pop culture," or "How will this system of magic change my life?". Questions like these need to be asked, because it helps you get clear on what's motivating you to develop a system of pop culture magic. Critical thinking will also help you understand a very important fact: When you develop a system of magic and practice it, you are opening the door to having your life changed as a result of doing that work, and the changes will not always occur in the way you expect. You need to know that and accept it.

People sometimes think that because they are creating and developing a system of magic they have complete control over it, but the truth is that it isn't just you creating and developing the system. It's you and the spiritual contacts you work with. And if

---

[14] As a rule of thumb spirits, pop culture and traditional, typically don't care about sex or romance. They primarily see sex as a means to deepen a connection, as opposed to anything more significant or romantic.

you happen to create a system where it's just magical techniques, you nonetheless will find that working with those techniques will still bring changes you didn't expect. I make that point because you need to go into this with your eyes open as to what you are doing.

You need to apply spiritual discernment and critical thinking to your work in creating and develop your magic system. Spiritual discernment will help you question the nature of the relationships you're developing with your pop culture spirits, so that you can be sure it's not all in your head and just wishful thinking. You want to test and verify your experiences with the spirits you work with and spiritual discernment will help with that. Critical thinking will help you ask the tough questions about why you're doing what you're doing. It'll help you examine each of your workings and the system overall to make sure the system works and also to fix any issues that come up.

How do I pick the right pop culture to work with?

Some of you may already know what pop culture you'll work with, but some of you won't. I want to share with you a few criteria you can apply, and a personal example from my own experience. I love it when I come across pop culture that sucks me in enough to make me want to work with it in a magical context. Recently I picked up the game *Horizon Zero Dawn* and instantly fell in love with the story and the heroine.

There isn't an overt system of magic at work in the game, and I'm not looking for one from it, but the main character Aloy is a compelling one who has to face her own fears in order to explore the world she is in. She's methodical about her exploration and always open to learning more and asking questions. When in a battle situation, she's strategical and tactical, able to assess a situation and figure out the best response. In short, she's a perfect example of a well-fleshed out character that can be worked with as a pop culture spirit.

I'm very picky about what pop culture I'll work with in a magical context. While I enjoy a lot of different pop culture, if I choose to work with one in a magical sense, there's one of three criteria that have to be met.

The first criteria is that the character has to be compelling and real enough to be a spirit I want to work with. Not all pop culture characters feel that way to me. What makes a character real for me is partially based on the character in and of themselves, and partially based on the connection. Do I feel like I can have a conversation with this character? Do I feel this character can teach me something?

The second criteria is actually kind of related to the first. It's the acknowledgement that sometimes a character will pick you to work with. Sometimes you are chosen and you have to decide if you'll really refuse that gift. I never have. I'll admit in the case of Aloy that criteria 1 and 2 came together. She picked me as much as I picked her.

The third criteria applies specifically to pop culture systems of magic you may be drawing on. The pop culture needs to have a well fleshed out system of magic that could be adapted to actual magical practice and theory. You may find that you can't apply everything from the pop culture magic to your actual system, but you ideally should be able to take the concepts and ideas and find a way to turn them into techniques. For example, way back when I really got into *Dragonball Z* for a while and what I found fascinating was how the show described working with the Chi. I still can't throw a visible Kamehaha, but what that show helped me do was apply the concepts of chi manipulation to what I was already doing. I developed a much better understanding of Chi work as a result and later on when I started learning about Taoism, the information I'd picked up in *DBZ* came full circle.

In the case of *Horizon Zero Dawn*, it's the character of Aloy that is compelling. There is a mythology around her and of course there is also the actions and thoughts of the character as well. My decision to work with her is also prompted by my own internal work and going into spaces where I feel very vulnerable. Having a fearless explorer at my side who knows how to read the environment and chart the best possible path is a boon.

Conclusion

I've treated this first chapter as an FAQ, in order to explore what I consider the basic, ground level questions people should ask before they even begin to put together a system of magic (pop culture or otherwise). From here, we're going to delve into more advanced topics that will help us actually put a system of magic together. Before we do that, here are a few exercises to help you get prepared for this work.

1. Make a list of the pop culture universes you might want to develop a system of magic around. Then write down why you want to develop a system of magic around those universes. I want you to also take a critical look at each one and ask if it's possible to develop a pop culture magic system for it.

2. What is your definition of a system of magic? What do you need in order to create a system of magic? Write your answers down.

Finally visit the Pop Culture Magick Facebook group and share your answers in the group. Please use the hashtag #PCMsystems so I can find your answers

Did you know I also write Fiction?

At Imagine Your Reality, I invite you to explore my fantastical worlds of fiction and make them part of your reality. Whether you're following the adventures of a superhero who's learning how to fly or rooting for a support analyst as he fights off zombies, my hope is that my stories will entertain you and take you to a fantastical place. I write fiction with a twist, because I like to surprise my readers and that's exactly what you'll get with my writing.

That's what Imagine Your Reality is about and I invite you to take a glimpse of the fantastic and read my free novella The Zombie Apocalypse Convenience Store, which explores what happens when a convenience store clerk has to survive the zombie apocalypse.

Visit Imagineyourreality.com to get the free story and get notifications when I publish my fiction.

Get the Magical Journals of Taylor Ellwood

My magical journals are a collection of articles, blog entries, and personal musings about magic, where I share my work in progress. If you want to learn how magic works, reading these journals can show you the work in progress of a magician, which can be a valuable to way to learn magic. You can pick them up at any e-book retailer. To learn more visit http://www.magicalexperiments.com/magical-journals-of-taylor-ellwood

Learn how Pop Culture Magic Works

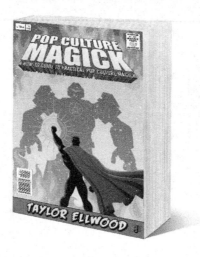

Magick for geeks! *Pop Culture Magick* is about a new approach to doing magick. Taylor Ellwood recognize that in this day and age the truly flexible magician is the magician who adapts with the times. *Pop Culture Magick* is a reflection of this need for adaptation. Ideas for practical magick can come from many unusual sources and pop culture is one such source. *Pop Culture Magick* walks you through how to apply pop culture to your magical practices.

Available in print and on any digital e-book format. Visit https://www.magicalexperiments.com/pop-culture-magic-series/to get your copy today!

Learn how Space/Time Magic works

Learn how to apply the elements of time, space, memory, and imagination to your magical practice so you that can possibilities into realities. If you've struggled with results based magic, or just want to learn how space/time magic can become another part of your practical magic process, Taylor will show you how to turn time and space into your allies so that you can turn possibilities into reality. Available at https://www.magicalexperiments.com/space-time-magic-series